90 YEARS OF GRACE

REFLECTIONS FROM MY JOURNEY

MORE PRAISE FOR 90 YEARS OF GRACE

REV. DR. DAVID OGINDE
Bishop, Christ is the Answer Ministries (CITAM)

Every once in a while God raises up a man or woman who truly touches the lives of many. Though I did not know him early enough, the short time I knew and worked with Mzee Ondeng', I was left with no doubt that he was a deep and sincere man of God. But, after going through this reflection, like Queen Sheba said to Solomon, I can say to Mzee Ondeng', "Indeed, not even half was told me; in wisdom and wealth you have far exceeded the report I heard." Herein is a rich reflection over an ordinary life, lived in an extraordinary way, under the guiding hand of God. It's honest, hilarious, yet deeply inspiring.

REV. MERVYN THOMAS,
Former Senior Pastor, Nairobi Pentecostal Church

For 13 years, from 1970 to 1983, when Sheila and I pastored the Nairobi Pentecostal Church in Nairobi, Kenya, East Africa, it was our joy to work alongside Richard Ondeng in his various capacities on the Church board, and his other responsibilities. During those years, on a number of occasions, the President of Kenya, His Excellency Daniel arap Moi, with many of his cabinet members attended the church Sunday morning services. The city of Nairobi was touched by the Spirit of the Living God and so many people came to accept Jesus as their Saviour and Lord through the many ministries of Nairobi Pentecostal Church.

Richard and Dinah and their lovely family were such a blessing to us both and our family, and to this day we have numerous fond memories of our relationship with them which remain in our hearts.

Of special remembrance to us, is the time Richard was the Chairman of the 13th Pentecostal World Conference, which took place in Nairobi in September of 1982, when delegates from all over the world came to this great Conference, with Richard and the committee giving expert leadership and guidance.

Richard was a good family man in every respect, yet strict, a man of influence who believed in tough love. He was renowned, admired, respected, wise and careful in all his dealings. He did so much for Nairobi Pentecostal Church and its congregation and could open doors that others could not, and we admire him to his day. His wisdom, knowledge and experience were such a tremendous help to us and to the Board of Deacons of the church.

Thank you Richard. God bless you and your family all of whom we love and admire to this day.

REV. MURRAY CORNELIUS,
PAOC Assistant Superintendent for International Missions

As part of the generation that stands on the shoulders of men and women like Richard and Dinah Ondeng', reading 90 Years of Grace reminds me of the importance of roots and legacy. Reading about familiar places (Valley Road, Nyang'ori and Kereri) and familiar people (Jack Lynn, John McBride, Mervyn Thomas and Dennis White) was more than just a journey down memory lane. There are important principles of leadership to be mined as we walk with a servant leader through his memories of faithful service to the Lord and to his church.

I was only 10 years old when the Ondeng's joined Nairobi Pentecostal Church. I know that my Father, Bill Cornelius, trusted this man implicitly as they worked together to navigate the relationship between the PAOC and the PAG. I recall the dignity, the grace, the wisdom and the demonstration of Christian character that was always on display. To borrow a phrase from Eugene Peterson, Richard Ondeng' demonstrates what 'A Long Obedience in the Same Direction' means.

REV. PROF. GODFREY M. NGURU
Former Vice Chancellor for Daystar University, St. Paul's University and Pan Africa Christian University

In this well written and easy to read book, Richard Ondeng demonstrates his good understanding of the Bible and his willingness to unwavering live by its teaching. His faith is thoroughly integrated in his life and work. You see this in his attitude to marriage, family and in any working situation that he ever found himself. Richard looked at every job he did or any position that he held as a calling from God.

His achievements, and they were many , are all attributed to the grace of God. With this conviction he gave himself fully to every job that he did. In this way Richard demonstrated the true meaning of servant leadership not just through what he wrote in this book but by the way he has lived. Those of us who know him or have had the opportunity to work with Richard can attest to that.

Consequently he has made immense contribution to the development of education and growth of the church in Kenya. He has made an indelible mark and should be emulated by all who desire to live out God's purposes in their lives.

In this book Richard comes through as a very humble but also very firm on issues that he believes in. This is very clear when he has had to deal with issues of traditions and culture particularly where they come into conflict with his Christian belief. This book is a must read for all who desire to follow Christ in their lives, those in leadership and those aspiring to be leaders in both Christian and secular settings.

REV. BONIFES ADOYO
Bishop Emeritus, Christ is the Answer Ministries (CITAM)

Brother Richard Ondeng's life spans the generation that transited from the colonization to the Africanization of Kenya. Through his wisdom and deep insight, he navigated the institutions associated with him to great heights of success and glory. When he speaks, people listen attentively and wait in silence for his council and afterwards nobody speaks again."Wisdom resides with the aged, and with length of days, understanding".

REV. HELEN MACMINN
Pentecostal Assemblies of Canada (PAOC) Kenya Team Leader

A truly inspiring account of the personal faith journey of a visionary servant leader. It is the story of one who stands out as a pillar of the church in Kenya. On reading this lovely book one can only conclude that the gospel pioneers he celebrates were enormously grateful for his wise counsel and dedicated leadership in the work of the Lord.

REV. DR. GEORGE E. WANJAU
Former Moderator, Presbyterian Church of East Africa (PCEA)

God has used Richard Ondeng in untold ways to leave a positive footprint in the lives of very many people, not just in Kenya, but in many parts of the world. We worked together during his years with CCEA and later in NCCK where I had the privilege of serving as Chairman. More recently, we have walked together as Trustees of the Lois Bulley Bursary Fund, a scheme for supporting the education of girls from poor backgrounds in Kenya. Through these many years of working together, I have come to know Richard as an authentic, sincere and prayerful man with a heart for service. In his book, 90 Years of

Grace, he gives us a little glimpse into the journey in which God led him to be the exceptional servant leader that he is. I am so proud to have been part of this journey. May God use this little book to inspire and bless generations to come.

RICHARD O. ONDENG'

90
YEARS OF
GRACE

REFLECTIONS FROM MY JOURNEY

Published by:

Lead Africa Publishers, a division of Lead Africa Institute, P. O. Box 18061 Nairobi, Kenya 00100
www.leadafrica.net

Printed in Nairobi, Kenya
Design and layout: Garo Designs
Editing: Diane Omondi
Cover photo: Pete Ondeng
First printing: November 2015

ISBN: 978-9966-094-14-8

CONTENTS

DEDICATION

This book is dedicated to my wife Dinah and to our eight children, Rhoda, Pete, Mary, Karin, Paul, Jim, Timothy and Phillip.

The Lord bless you and keep you; the Lord make His face shine upon you, and be gracious to you; the Lord lift up His countenance upon you, and give you peace. Amen.

ACKNOWLEDGMENTS

I wish I could do more than just say "thank you" to the many people who have been a part of my journey and who have blessed me, challenged me, loved me and helped me in so many ways. As much as I would like to acknowledge each one personally, I feel that it would be an impossible task.

In this late hour of my life, I have decided to write this book as a testament of God's favor, which was often demonstrated through the people that He brought into my life. My family, relatives, teachers, friends, colleagues, neighbours, associates and, yes, even those who worked against me; all played a part in shaping me into the person I am today. This book is more about them than it is about me

Unfortunately, many of those with whom I served and worked over the years have passed on. I wish it were possible for me to go back and thank each one of them personally. But I take comfort in knowing that I will meet many of them in heaven when my time comes to go to that eternal home.

Forward
By Rev. Dennis E. White

Richard Ondeng's book, 90 Years of Grace – Reflections From My Journey, is indeed an enlightening and gripping account of God's miraculous and amazing grace at work in the life of a humble recipient.

My wife Esther and I were privileged to be closely associated with Mr. Ondeng' during our fourteen years and four months of pastoral ministry with Nairobi Pentecostal church.

Richard's vital and valuable contribution to the Kenyan society, to NPC, and to us personally without doubt played an incalculable role in the growth and expansion of the church.

Through my many interactions with the author I was led to view him as hard working, disciplined, well organized, a stickler for detail and one who gave himself fully to whatever task he was doing. I also found him to be a good listener and one who never failed to praise a job well done.

As Richard Ondeng's brother in Christ I was always delighted to be around him. He exuded certain qualities worthy of emulation. However, since he was so private and dignified, I felt that I would be trespassing if I were to ask him about the circumstances in life to which he attributed the grace of God that was so wonderfully used to fashion him into the man we knew.

Well, this volume answers that question and is quite the revelation. Richard's candid transparency shows what the grace of God can do to a sinner saved by grace.

I pray that these well-documented and honest reflections of this influential and highly respected Kenyan education professional, yet also a genuine Christian gentleman, would provoke every reader to personally experience the power of God's grace available to all who would trust Jesus Christ as personal Saviour and choose to live under His Lordship.

In conclusion, I was overtaken by surprise when asked by Richard Ondeng' if I would consider honoring him by writing the foreword to this book. The idea that this man, who interacted with so many notable religious leaders and well stationed educators over his many years, would ask me to make this contribution to his book 90 Years of Grace – Reflections From My Journey is indeed an honour I deeply treasure.

Rev. Dennis White

PREFACE

This book is not an autobiography. It is simply a collection of my thoughts and reflections from the life that God has allowed me to live on this earth. As I approach my 90th birthday, I am so aware that my days are numbered. With each passing day, I am reminded that I am living on borrowed time. *Psalms 90:10* says

> *The days of our lives are seventy years;*
> *And if by reason of strength they are eighty years,*
> *Yet their boast is only labour and sorrow;*
> *For it is soon cut off, and we fly away.*

In Kenya, it is said that life expectancy is around 50 years for men. If that is true, then I have lived almost two life-times. I do not know why God would choose to give me this extra time on earth. What I do know is that, to whom much is given, much is expected. Even at my ripe old age, I am expected to give all that I can and all that I have for the sake of the Kingdom.

The Bible says in James 4:14, *"You do not even know what will happen tomorrow! What is your life? You are a mist that appears for a little while and then vanishes."* Praise be to God that I have the assurance of where I will go when the time comes for me to vanish.

I have lived a full life, and I must say that I have seen the faithfulness of God in real and practical ways. It would be quite a shame if I were to go to my grave without sharing some of those testimonies – even if they were to encourage just one person. Testifying to God's faithfulness and encouraging others is what this book is all about. It is both a personal testimony and my word of encouragement and blessing to those whom God will allow to read this book.

Looking Ahead

Let me say just how amazing the view from behind looks when one reaches the age of 90. The world has changed in many ways during my lifetime. Yet there are some things that will never change. For one, God's word does not change. He Himself is the same, yesterday, today and forever. He does not change with time. And it is through the prism of His unchanging love that I choose to look back over my life and try to distill some lessons that may be of help to someone in the years to come – in the event that Christ's return is delayed.

If I had to live my life all over again, there are many things that I would do differently. I made many mistakes along the way, and there were some choices I made that I would not repeat today. The Christian life is not an easy life. There is no man or woman who does not slip and fall or lose his or her way at some point in the forest of life. I can testify to many stumbles that drove me back to my knees to ask God for forgiveness. Amazingly, He always did forgive. And even now, He forgives me when I confess my sins to Him.

My being a sinner does not hinder me from speaking about righteousness. If anything, it gives me an even greater urgency to testify to the goodness of God who never gave up on me, even in those times when I turned my back on Him. More than anything else, my testimony is about His grace. It is by His grace that, at this moment, I still have breath. With that breath, I choose to praise Him. May God's blessing and favor be with you and all those who will read this testimony.

Richard

CHAPTER 1

A SAVIOUR AND HEALER

*For it is by grace you have been saved, through faith--and this
is not from yourselves, it is the gift of God, not by works, so that
no one can boast.*

Ephesians 2: 8-9

I could not begin to count the number of evangelistic church services
or crusades I have attended, and how many times I have listened to
preachers making altar calls. The altar call has become more or less
a routine part of the evangelical Christian church service. It usually
takes place at the end of the service, and the routine is quite predictable.

"If you want to accept Jesus as your personal Saviour," the preacher
usually says, "please lift up your hand and put it back down." After a
few minutes, those who raised their hands are asked to stand up. And
finally, once they are standing, these same people are asked to come to
the front of the church to be prayed for.

On many such occasions, the preacher will ask the responders to repeat some words after him, and thereupon, he declares the people "saved". I have often wondered to myself how many of the people responding to these altar calls really understand that salvation is so much more than just reciting some words that have originated with an evangelist. How many of them walk away from those services understanding what it really means to commit one's life to Jesus?

My own salvation was quite dramatic. When I gave my life to Christ after many years of denying Him, I did so knowing that, with God, there is no middle ground. You are either a follower of Christ or you are not. I will talk more about some of the struggles I faced in my journey as a Christian, especially when I found myself caught between the demands of my faith as a Christian and those of the culture into which I was born, in a later chapter.

An Invisible, Guiding Hand

Looking back on my early years, I cannot help but marvel at how God literally plucked me out of darkness and brought me into His Kingdom of light. Perhaps the word "pluck" is not completely accurate, because mine was a long journey of resistance and rebellion before I finally submitted to the authority of Christ over my life.

My first encounter with Christianity was in 1935. I was then only about eight years old. My step grandmother had been converted to Catholicism, which was slowly taking root in the western part of Kenya where I grew up. The only other organized Christian group that was visible in that area at the time was the Church Missionary Society (CMS).

My father forbade me and my younger brother from getting involved with either group. However, he did allow me to accompany my aging step grandmother to her church, which was about six kilometers from where we lived. I would walk her to church on Saturdays for confession and then again on Sundays for Holy Communion. I did not understand the rituals and ceremonies that I saw my step grandmother going through, but I remember being fascinated and curious about what they all meant.

In June 1936, my father, who was then around 50 years of age, acceded to pleas from various people from the growing Anglican Church to send me to school. He had struggled with the decision for two reasons. First, he knew that my going to school would pull me into the Christian religion, and he was firmly against my joining the church. Secondly, as his first son, it was my duty to take care of the family's small herd of cows, and Dad was eager to transfer this burden to me as soon as I was mature enough to manage it. In granting me permission to go to school, Dad set a condition that I would have to arrive back home while it was still daylight so that I could spend a few hours every day taking care of the cows. It was important to him that I did not turn my back on this responsibility.

I was excited about going to school. I had been quietly envious of a few other boys from our village that had gone to school, but I had never imagined that my father would allow me to go.

The school that would serve as my entry point into formal education was run by the Church Mission Society (CMS). The school, then called Usingo Sector School, was approximately four miles away from home. Young as I was, I knew that a new world was about to open up for me. I was eager, and determined to do well. What I did not know was that my journey into Christendom was also just beginning.

In retrospect, I can see how God gently guided my steps and drew me to Himself. The Bible says that it is by grace that a man is saved. It is not by our works or anything that we can boast about. Over time, I would come to learn that God's wish is that no one should perish.

I would also come to learn that, while His hand of grace is extended to all, it is by choice that each individual person is saved. It is also by choice that a person is not saved. It would take me several years before I would finally make the choice to submit my life to Christ.

A week or so after joining the CMS primary school, I learned that I would have to attend Sunday school. Attendance was mandatory. I also found out that all students were expected to go through the Anglican confirmation process. The confirmation process is designed to lead a person to become a member of the Anglican Church. It involves doctrinal training and preparation for Baptism and Holy Communion.

While keeping much of this away from my father, I dutifully enrolled in the confirmation process and entered the first stage, which was then referred to as the "Seeking Class". I went through the stage mechanically, and passed the tests that were given. As it turned out, many of those who took the test with me failed. Those of us who passed were allowed to go to the next stage, called "Promise". This second stage involved a lot of memorization of scripture, which I did quite well. After one year, I again took an exam and I passed. I then moved on to the next stage, which was the "Baptism" class.

I sat for the Baptism test in August 1938 along with a small group of other young people. This time, only two of us passed – I and a lady called Mariam. I was now qualified to be baptized. As was the Anglican practice then, baptism of Africans involved the assignment of a name from a character in the Bible. For reasons that I cannot explain, the name given to me was Richard. From that day on, I would be considered a "Christian", and my first name would be Richard and not Onyango, the latter being the name that my parents had given me.

A Bumpy Journey

The one word that best describes my experience as a student from the time I entered primary school to the time I finished my post secondary training as a teacher is "bumpy". I will talk about that journey in some detail in chapter three. For now, let me just say that the things that I achieved were not because of who I was, but in spite of who I was. As I grew up and interacted more and more with the world outside of my village, I became cynical about Christianity. Although I did not show it on the outside, I developed a negative attitude toward the church, which I increasingly associated with European dominance over us Africans.

Throughout my high school and subsequent teachers' training years, I stood out as a good student, a star athlete and a leader among my peers. I also grew in my self confidence. Over time, this gave way to a certain arrogance that would, on many occasions, land me into conflict situations. In many ways, I was a non-conformist. But for some reason, when it came to Christianity, I conformed and played along for years, not wanting to be seen as a "sinner". I attended church and went through the rituals, including communion, but none of those things had any personal meaning to me.

When I completed my teachers' training course at the then highly acclaimed Kagumo Teachers Training College, I earned my diploma and prepared myself to enter the world of employment. It was gratifying to find that, with my good pass, many schools were prepared to offer me a teaching job. After reviewing all of my options, the choice came down to two Western Kenya schools, both of which I had attended. The first was Nyang'ori Junior Secondary School, owned and operated by the Pentecostal Assemblies of Canada (PAOC). The second was Maseno School, a highly rated CMS school. In the end, I chose to accept the offer by the PAOC to join the teaching staff at Nyang'ori Junior.

I have often wondered how my life would have turned out if I had taken the job in Maseno. Once again, I believe it was the hand of Jesus, the Good Shepherd, which gently nudged me and led me along His path of righteousness – for His own name's sake. It was at Nyang'ori where I met the girl who was to later become my wife and mother to our eight children. But most importantly, it was at Nyang'ori where I came face to face with the Lord Jesus and made the most important decision of my life: to accept Him as my Lord and Saviour.

Jesus Knocking On My Door

In accepting the Nyang'ori offer, I had put a condition to Rev. Brown, the missionary Principal who had interviewed me for the job. My condition was that I would be given different accommodation from the dilapidated staff housing where the African teachers were housed. Rev. Brown had acceded to my demand, but I could see the concern in his face, and I knew that my entrance would stir some discontent among the other staff members.

In January of 1949, I moved into a guest house at the compound of the Nyang'ori Secondary School Principal and started my teaching career. As expected, the show of preferential treatment toward me by the Principal did not go down well with the other staff. My arrogance did not help matters much, and I quickly found myself isolated and rejected by the people who would be my colleagues.

Rev. Brown was aware of the animosity that his decision had created, but he remained supportive and never wavered in his confidence in me. That first evening, he took me around to meet the staff, some of whom had taught me when I had attended the school years before. The reception I received was very cold.

The next day, at my first staff meeting, a big argument erupted over the teaching timetable. The contention was that the schedule was unworkable, and some teachers were overworked while others were under-worked. The discussion went back and forth, and no one seemed prepared to take up the task of rethinking the schedule and coming up with an alternative. I was silent through most of the discussion, wondering what all the fuss was about. Toward the end of the meeting, I offered to take up the task of reworking the timetable.

Everyone looked at me sceptically, but no one objected to giving me the assignment. This was my first opportunity. I poured myself into the task and, by that afternoon, I had resolved the issues that had caused the whole uproar. The icy reception that I had received thawed slightly, and I slowly gained credibility among my colleagues.

Over the next several years, I would prove myself to be a faithful and diligent worker. In 1951, I was promoted to the position of Deputy Principal, serving under Mr. Arthur Rosenau. Mr. Rosenau was the missionary who had taken over from Rev. Brown when Rev. Brown had chosen to take up other full time mission work in the region. By the time I was taking on this new job, I had moved out of the Principal's guest house and into my own house – a relatively large, two-bedroom brick house at the edge of the school compound.

I was a strict disciplinarian, and my students scored highly on their exams. The PAOC missionaries with whom I worked treated me with respect. In spite of my ambivalence toward their "loud" evangelical brand of Christianity, I was accepted and felt genuinely appreciated.

That same year, I was assigned to take over leadership of the school's athletics program. Things were going well for me. My future looked bright and I felt unstoppable. There was just one nagging issue that sometimes kept me awake at night. My closest friend, the man who would later be the best man in my wedding, had just given his life to Christ.

Owen Gumba was a friend closer than a brother. I had been instrumental in getting him a job at Nyang'ori, and everyone knew that we were inseparable. Owen's salvation was a direct challenge to me, but I refused to budge. God was knocking on my door, but I would not let Him in.

My Turning Point

If there is one thing that we tend to take for granted, and which God sometimes uses to remind us of our mortality, it is our health. When it comes to sickness, no man or woman can claim immunity.

My first bout with a life threatening illness came when everything seemed to be going so well. It started off with a slight cold, which I ignored, and which progressed in ways that I could not have predicted. In my stubbornness, I made some foolish decisions and pressed on with my work including an ill-advised trip with our school football team to Kakamega High School.

When we got back from the trip, I was immediately hospitalized in Kisumu and then later transferred to the Maseno Mission Hospital. There, it was discovered that my cold had developed into pneumonia. Due to my negligence, the pneumonia had also progressed into another disease - pleurisy, a disease that involves inflammation of the tissue layers (pleura) lining the lungs and inner chest wall. I was informed by Dr. Leech, the missionary doctor attending to me, that there was no cure for the disease. "Only God can cure you," he told me.

That, to me, was a death sentence. I was weak, depressed and helpless. I could hardly eat, leave alone do anything else. I was discharged and, for the next five months, I would be virtually bed-ridden in my house, merely waiting to die.

People came and went. My friend Owen would encourage me, but I could see in his eyes that he too was struggling to remain positive. My mind began to go blank. I stopped caring about things that used to be so important to me. I didn't want to die, but there was nothing I could do to stop what seemed to be inevitable.

And then it happened. I will never forget that day. It was Friday, the 9th of May, 1952. Arthur Rosenau, the Principal, together with his wife, Edna, and June Deacon, another missionary on the teaching staff, came to the house to pray for me. Arthur and June had been coming to see me almost every day for five months to pray for me and to persuade me to accept Jesus as my Lord and Saviour. Evidently, they had understood that I was a "practicing" Christian, but not a "born again" Christian. It was an interesting distinction that I pondered over as I lay on my bed, waiting to die.

Throughout that particular week, Arthur and June had been trying to convince me to come with them to an evangelistic crusade that was being held at the church compound of the mission station. The week-long crusade was an annual event organized by PAOC, and each year a special guest evangelist was invited. That year, the evangelist was a South African Pentecostal preacher called Nicholas Bengu.

I had repeatedly declined the invitation from Arthur and his wife to attend the crusade. I just did not have the strength. I appreciated their concern, but I had lost the will to live. Nothing really made sense to me anymore. I just wanted to be left alone.

"Today is the last day of the crusade," Arthur said to me on that memorable Friday. I looked at the three missionaries blankly and wished that they would stop disturbing me. Rosenau pleaded with me to come and let the evangelist pray for my healing. "God wants to heal you, Richard. Why don't you come and let God do a miracle for you?"

"A miracle? What miracle? Why would God do a miracle for me?" These were the thoughts that passed through my mind. And just then, the first miracle happened. The door to my heart, which had been shut tightly, suddenly loosened. For the first time, I wished that what these noisy missionaries were saying could be true. Reluctantly, I nodded my head and whispered that I would come with them.

It took me some time to get dressed. I had not been out of the house for almost five months. It took a lot of effort to walk. Arthur and Edna supported me and I slowly got into the car. June drove the car gently to the crusade, which was less than a kilometer away from my house. When we got to the tent where the crusade was being held, I was helped out of the car and motioned to them to let me walk unassisted.

It was a long, slow but steady walk to the front. I could feel every eye in the place looking at me. Many of the students and staff had not seen me for months. I had become thin and gaunt. Everyone knew that I was terminally ill, and that I was only marking time.

I sat down in the front row and tried to concentrate on what the preacher was saying. The sermon was from Hebrews 9:27:

> *"And as it is appointed unto men once to die, but after this the judgment."*

I listened to the preacher talking about the finality of death and the irreversible outcome of the choice we make before we die. I knew he was talking to me. I began to shake as he closed his Bible and made an appeal to those in the crowd who wanted to accept Christ as Saviour. I did not wait for anyone to prompt me. I knew for certain that God had brought this man to Nyang'ori for me. I stood up and walked unsteadily, but with great determination, to the front and repeated the "sinners' prayer" after the evangelist.

I felt tears coming to my eyes. I was saved. Now I would not have to fear death. I stood there with my head bowed, wondering why it had taken me so many years to respond to Christ.

And then the voice of the preacher came again – this time with an intensity that startled me. "If you are sick or in pain, put your hand on the place where you are hurting, and I will pray for God to heal you," he said.

I didn't know what part of my body to touch. I was sick all over. I was like a dead man walking. I put my right hand on my chest and listened as he prayed. I wanted so badly to believe that I would be healed, but my mind was full of doubt. God saw the desire of my heart, and He heard my feeble prayer. In that moment – without a shadow of doubt – I knew I had been healed. Almost involuntarily, I bent down to touch my knee. I had not been able to bend for months. My soul was suddenly flooded with joy. God had saved me. And then He had healed me.

I was still weak, and I knew that I would have to work on restoring the weight and strength that I had lost. But that was nothing. I was a new person, and a new journey was about to begin.

CHAPTER 2

GROWING PAINS

And we know that all things work together for good to them
that love God, to them who are the called according to his
purpose.

Romans 8:28

As a Christian who has walked with the Lord for over six decades, I have learned many things. Among the things I have learned is just how limited I am and how big God is. My journey from childhood to maturity was marked with struggle, disappointment and frustration. As a human being, I cannot see the future, nor can I comprehend why things happen the way they do. What I do know is that God sees everything, including the things that are yet to come.

In the scripture I have quoted above, Romans 8:28, the Lord is saying that all things – not some things but all things – including my mistakes, my good and bad choices and my experiences – ultimately work together for good if I love the Lord and I endeavor to be aligned with His divine purpose.

This one scripture gives me great comfort when I look back on the many ups and downs of my life. God has a way of weaving all of these experiences, actions, decisions and thoughts into something good and pleasing to Him.

Needless to say, my salvation in 1952 was a major milestone and turning point in my journey. Leading up to that decision were many twists and turns that should not be looked at in isolation. These twists and turns worked together to shape my thinking and to bring me into alignment with God's purpose for my life.

A Rude awakening

In 1942, as I came to the end of my primary school education, I ran into the first of many obstacles that I would face in my academic journey. I had mistakenly assumed that, after primary school, I would automatically go to Maseno School, a prestigious CMS boys' school on the outskirts of Kisumu.

Maseno School is the oldest formal education school in Kenya. It was established in 1906 by missionaries, initially as a school for the children of African chiefs. Over the years, the school grew and attracted youthful boys from all over Western Kenya. Apart from reading and writing, students were taught various practical skills such as carpentry, tailoring, printing, building, and clerical work. Teacher training was introduced later to train teachers who would in turn teach new students. Those who studied at the school were tested at the end of their courses and awarded certificates.

A big part of Maseno's fame can be attributed to Mr. Edward Carey Francis, a man who came to Kenya as a missionary and teacher from Cambridge, UK. With the help of the colonial office, Carey Francis secured a job as Headmaster at Maseno School in December 1927, just as I reached my second birthday. During his tenure, Maseno School rose to become one of the most coveted schools in East Africa. His illustrious administration of the school attracted other teachers from Cambridge, and the school became an academic oasis in the region. Francis headed Maseno School from 1928 until 1940, the year before I was to complete my primary education and presumably go to Maseno.

My performance at the Anglican primary school that I was attending was quite good. For that reason alone, I had felt more or less assured that, upon completion, I would be accepted in Maseno School.

However, when the time came for me and my classmates to sit for the Common Entrance Examination, we were told that we would not be allowed to sit for the examination if we had not been confirmed as Anglicans. This announcement came to us as a shock because we had not been informed about this condition earlier. My spirit sank. I now knew that my chance to enter Maseno had been dashed.

The truth was that, while I had successfully undergone the various steps leading up to confirmation, I had actually boycotted the final series of classes because of 'bad blood' that had developed between me and the Catechism teacher. In my eyes, he was a hypocrite and I had decided that I would rather not be confirmed if it meant being taught for confirmation by him.

I now felt suddenly lost and confused. I knew that the man had withheld this information from me deliberately, and that now he was going to have the last laugh. Tears of anger and frustration welled up inside me. My chance to join Maseno School was about to slip through my fingers.

In my desperation, I went to see a CMS missionary who was in charge of the work in the area. The missionary, whose name was Canon Walter Edwin Owen, was a down-to-earth, friendly man who had taken time on a few occasions to talk with me, almost like a friend. I was too young then to fully appreciate that Canon. Owen, simple as he was actually quite a senior figure in the CMS hierarchy in East Africa. Some years earlier, he had been appointed to serve as the CMS Archdeacon of the entire Western Kenya diocese (then called Kavirondo).

At the time, Archdeacon Owen was responsible for organizing the new, rapidly expanding church among the Luo, Luhya, and Kalenjin peoples. I would later come to learn about his confrontations with the colonial administration for its discrimination against Africans. Archdeacon Owen was a very practical man who devoted much of his time to teaching our people how to run their own affairs and how to realize economic development.

When I approached him that morning in October 1941 with my dilemma, he looked at me with great concern in his eyes. It would be a shame, he told me, if I did not go to Maseno. He promised me that he would do whatever he could to see that I would not miss this opportunity.

I am not sure about all that happened behind the scenes, but through Archdeacon Owens' intervention, I was allowed to go on an intense, fast-track confirmation process that he administered personally. It mostly involved reading and a lot of memorization of scripture. At the end of one month, I was ready to be confirmed alongside other students who had gone through the normal year-long process. Naturally, my being allowed to take this shortcut to confirmation created some animosity among my fellow students, and it certainly did not endear me to the Head Teacher whom I had defied.

The following month, in December of that year, I took the entrance exam for Maseno School, and I did very well. I was one of 55 students from different schools in the region who passed the exam and thereby qualified for admission. It was a moment of pride for me, and I showed up for school in January 1942, unaware that my excitement was about to come crashing down.

What I did not know was that the school would only be able to take 45 of the 55 students, and ten of us would have to be distributed to other schools in the region. One month into the term, our entire class of 55 was told to line up outside one of the buildings. The then Principal of the school, a man called A. W. Mayor, proceeded to count us off from one end of the line to the other. When he reached the number 45, he stopped. He then informed us that this was a difficult decision, but that only the 45 students who were counted off would be able to remain in the school.

The ten of us were asked to pick a school by drawing a piece of paper from a bag. I was devastated, but I had no choice. I reached my hand into the bag and pulled out a folded piece of paper and opened it slowly. Written on the paper was Nyang'ori Junior Secondary School. With that turn of events, the Lord brought me into the circle of the Pentecostal Assemblies of Canada.

Looking back now, I do believe that the Lord led me in that direction for a reason, even though it was such a devastating blow to me as a young teenager. Nyang'ori's standard and reputation was nowhere near that of Maseno, and I felt as if I had just been robbed of my future.

I went to Nyang'ori with three other students who had also picked the school out of the bag. I smile now as I look back on that moment. There is no way I could have known at the time that I would one day come back to that same school as a teacher and eventually rise to be the first African Principal of the school.

My first year at Nyang'ori was harsh. It was a predominantly Luhya school, and I experienced a lot of ethnic discrimination. The older students at the school bullied me along with the few other Luo students who were also going to school there.

The Principal of the school at that time was a Canadian missionary called James Skinner, the late father of Rev. Bob Skinner. Mr. Skinner left the school shortly after I started, and his position was taken over by Rev. John McBride, another PAOC missionary who had just arrived from Canada.

Rev. McBride would later become the PAOC Field Director before eventually moving to Nairobi to lead a PAOC assembly that was just being started. The assembly was called the Pentecostal Evangelistic Centre (PEC). That assembly would eventually evolve into the Nairobi Pentecostal Church (NPC), a church that many years later would become more than just a home church for me and my family.

Who would have known then that I would one day come back to serve as the Principal of Nyang'ori Secondary School? Who would have known that Rev. John McBride would become my pastor in Nairobi almost 30 years later? The answer is: God knew all of those things. Looking back now, I can clearly see how He so cleverly wove the events of my journey together for a divine purpose that is so much bigger than I could ever fathom.

CHAPTER 3

CALLED TO TEACH

And he gave some, apostles; and some, prophets; and some, evangelists; and some, pastors and teachers; for the perfecting of the saints, for the work of the ministry, for the edifying of the body of Christ.

Ephesians 4:11-12

They say, "Once a teacher, always a teacher". The title, "japuonj", which means "teacher" in my mother tongue, or "mwalimu" in Kiswahili, has followed me all these years even though I stopped teaching back in the 1950s. In East Africa, the title is generally used to convey respect and to honor the holder of the title.

I was a teacher by profession, but I am also a teacher by calling. I feel that God gave me the gift of teaching, and I have had the privilege of teaching and counseling thousands of people throughout my life in very many different settings. As I have grown older, I have come to appreciate more and more the role of teaching as a means of transforming society.

To be honest, I did not set out to become a teacher. Like many other things in my life, my footsteps were guided. God uses different ways to lead us, and often times we see His hand only after the fact.

I spent three years at Nyang'ori Junior Secondary School, after which, through an interesting turn of events, I ended up being called back to Maseno to complete my secondary education. I felt that I had lost some ground due to the years at Nyang'ori, but I was happy nonetheless to be back where I felt I belonged.

In 1946, I completed secondary school. At that point, I had regained my self-confidence, and my goal was to go to the prestigious Alliance High School for the last two years of my 'O' levels. From there, my ambition was to proceed to Makerere College in Kampala. Makerere was, in those days, the most esteemed university college in all of East Africa.

Those were my plans. But as I would learn again and again during my life journey, we can make our plans but God holds the last word. As it turned out, I was not among the 16 people selected in my year to go to Alliance. Although the competition was indeed stiff, I felt at the time that I had been discriminated against in the selection process.

In my view, the cards had been stacked in favor of the children of the "Who's Who" in Kenya. They had an edge over village boys from obscure backgrounds, like me. I had performed very well academically and was actually in third position in my class. Yet, I did not make the cut into Alliance. I was told that Alliance High School wanted younger men, and because I had started school late, my age (20 years at the time) supposedly worked against me.

My world crashed again. Why was this happening to me? I felt discouraged and somewhat confused by what I felt was a blatant injustice. I found it difficult to refocus my mind to choose a new path from among several trades and professions that were being offered to those of us who were not accepted into Alliance.

There were basically four alternatives from which we could choose:

a) Go and work for the Colonial Government in some clerical position

b) Go to medical training school

c) Work for one of the state owned enterprises like the Railways or Post Office

d) Go for teachers' training.

After a bout of internal struggle, I decided that I would go to Nairobi to be trained as a medical nurse. However, my experience at the Training Centre would be short lived. My boss was an abrasive European woman who shouted at us constantly and never had a good word for anyone. For a full month, my job was to collect and hand-wash bed sheets that had been used by sick patients in the hospital. It was difficult enough to have to deal with human waste and blood from the patients every day, but I probably would have weathered it had it not been for that woman.

At the end of one tiring day, I brought in the laundry which I had washed in the morning, and the lady began shouting at me, telling me that I was not doing a good enough job. I looked at her and, at that moment, made up my mind that I would leave. I had been at the Centre for only one month, and I was quitting. At the end of the scolding session, I walked away quietly but resolutely. The next day, I would hand in my things and go back to my village in Siaya. I did not know what this would mean for my future, but all I knew was that I was not going to stay in that abusive environment.

For the next month or so, I would literally hang around in the village, making myself busy wherever I could. When I got bored, I walked over to the primary school where I had started my formal education. The Headmaster welcomed me and allowed me assist with teaching in some of the classes on a voluntary basis. Although I was not employed by the school, I found myself enjoying the work. Slowly, I began to settle back into the rhythm of the rural village.

Another Turning Point

And then it happened. My moment of transition came suddenly and without warning. It was a typical day in the village. I had washed some of my clothes and hung them on a nearby bush to dry. I had been wandering around a bit aimlessly, unsure about whether I should go over to the school that day or not.

As I stood there in our small compound next to my thatched mud hut, I heard the rumble of a motor vehicle coming in my direction. "Why in the world would a car be coming to our village?" I wondered. I ran out to see what this was about and found other children and youth from the village who had also come to the road with a similar curiosity.

The man driving the rugged Land Rover stepped down from the vehicle and asked for Richard Onyango. I stepped forward and identified myself. The man handed me a piece of paper and informed me that I had been accepted at Kagumo Teachers College. He had been sent to collect me, so I would need to pack my things and go with him immediately so as to catch the train in Kisumu that same afternoon.

It was a spiritual moment for me. I felt a rush of adrenalin as I ran to find my mother who was working somewhere in the small garden. She was a special woman, and I look back on her life with fond memories. Like many women in our village, she toiled endlessly to keep the family going. She was always the first to rise in the morning. Her routine included collecting water from the river, gathering firewood from the bushes around the village and working in our small garden.

Looking back, I can't help but feel a bit sorry for my mom. Like virtually everyone in her generation, she had no formal education. What she had was the education of life, which had molded her into a leader among her peers and a caring, sensitive woman who bore with dignity the weight of being a woman in Africa.

She walked barefoot, and her hands were calloused with years of hard labour. Over the years, as my mom would grow older, her back would eventually give way and constrict her to a permanent bent position that only added to the challenges that she faced.

I gave her the news of the visitor who had come with the car, and then I paused for her response. I respected and loved my mother, and I knew that she looked up to me, even in my youth, to help her in easing the economic burdens of the family. I never really discussed much about my schooling with her, and I imagine that even the concept and value of education was not something that she would have grasped easily.

A few of the families around our village had put their daughters into school, but for the most part, education was for boys. There was no way I could have known then that I would one day be a champion of girls' education.

Mom looked at me, and I suppose she could see the intensity in my eyes. "Go and catch one of the big chickens," she said to me. It was her way of giving me a fitting send off. The man at the car had told me that we needed to leave quickly. But despite his suggestion, we would have to wait for my mother to gather some firewood, start a small fire and prepare a meal for me and the visitor. It was a painfully slow and tedious process, but looking back, I am glad that we waited and shared that special moment with my dad, my mom and my younger brother, Martin.

After a hurried lunch, I took my few clothes and got into the car. The driver told me that we were running late, but that he would try his best to make it to the train station on time. As we rumbled down the bumpy road to Kisumu, he explained to me what had happened that led to my personal invitation to Kagumo.

Apparently, Mr. A. W. Mayor, the then Principal of Maseno High School, had been told about my having walked out of the medical school to go back to the village. The driver explained that the Principal had gone out of his way to get me admitted into Kagumo Teachers Training College, then a highly regarded colonial government institution for training teachers.

I really don't know what led Mr. Mayor to put such effort into getting me into Kagumo. To be honest, I was sure that he did not like me. But here I was, in a car speeding into a fresh new season of my life because of him. What can I say except "praise be to God"? I can see now how the Lord guided my footsteps and opened doors for me even when I least deserved it.

We arrived in Kisumu shortly after 2 pm and found, to our dismay, that the train had just left. I remember my heart sinking. How was I possibly going to explain to anyone that I had missed my opportunity because I had to catch a chicken and wait for it to be cooked?

We walked over to the office of the Provincial Education Officer (PEO) and conjured up a story about why we had missed the train. We pleaded to be allowed to get on the train the next day, and to my joy, the officer agreed. I spent the rest of the day and that night at the home of my uncle who lived in Kisumu. On the following day, I arrived at the station on time and boarded the train.

The train took me to Nairobi where I boarded another train headed for Nanyuki in Central Kenya. I was exhausted when I finally made my way to the Kagumo campus. It was a Friday, and I remember feeling disoriented because the term had begun almost two months earlier; the rest of the student body had already established their rhythm. I needed to organize myself and settle down quickly if I was going to catch up to the rest of the class.

On the following Monday morning, on what was to be my first day in the class, I was informed that we would be going out to various local schools for teaching practice. The teacher who had organized the various groups and given out the assignments was a European lady called Ms. Hockley.

Given my lateness, I was obviously not prepared for this exercise, but Ms. Hockley placed me in one of the groups. Together we proceeded to the school to which that group had been assigned.

Ms. Hockley sat in the class as I was teaching, and she clearly was not happy with my performance. After the class, she called me aside and dressed me down, using harsh and abusive language. The following week, she wrote a letter to the Principal. In that letter, she effectively stated that I did not have what it took to be a teacher.

Once again, it seemed like I was staring at a "brick wall". I found myself going through the same emotions that I had experienced at the medical school. I was upset and hurt by the way I had been thrown into the teaching practice without preparation, and by how I was being handled unfairly.

Looking back now, I believe that God was preparing me for many challenges that I would face in years to come as a leader. I was proud and hot-tempered, and God was teaching me humility. If I was going to make it, I would need to climb down from my self-exalted position and focus on the task before me. Although I did not understand it at the time, I was being put through the fire of testing and purification for service to God.

The day after Ms. Hockley wrote the disparaging letter about me, I walked over to the Principal's office to register my own complaint about how I felt mistreated. Rev. Richard Lockhart turned out to be a Godsend. He was not only mature, calm and reassuring, but he effectively took me under his wing and told me not to worry about anything.

I was so many years younger than Rev. Lockhard, and yet he treated me like a friend. Over the two years that I would be at Kagumo, he and his wife would come to represent the good that I had always yearned to see in my leaders. They were firm but encouraging, and related to me in a personal way. His wife never tired of reminding me jokingly that I needed to behave well because I was carrying the name of her husband, Richard.

The two years at the college were memorable years. The time went by so fast. I remember saying 'goodbye' to my good friend, Owen Gumba. Owen had left Maseno School a year after me and joined me at the Kagumo Teachers College. I would later convince him to join me at Nyang'ori as a teacher. Our friendship would continue to grow, and years later, we would end up being best men in each other's weddings.

CHAPTER 4

A FELLOWSHIP OF BELIEVERS

And let us consider how we may spur one another on toward love and good deeds. Let us not give up meeting together, as some are in the habit of doing, but let us encourage one another--and all the more as you see the Day approaching.

Hebrews 10:24-25

ollowing my acceptance of Jesus as Lord and Saviour at the 1952 PAOC crusade in Nyang'ori I found myself faced with demands from other Christians who wanted me to join this or that fellowship. I had always been a very independent person, and I highly valued my privacy. I must confess that there was also an element of pride in me that made it difficult for some people to get along with me. My coming to Christ was a challenge to these ways, and I was not sure just how I was going to cope.

My good friend Owen, who was also teaching at Nyang'ori, had accepted Christ some months before me, and he was among the people who were badgering me about my need for fellowship. Owen had become part of the so called East African Revival fellowship that had been sweeping across East Africa. I had known about this movement for some time, but like with many other things related to Christianity, I had kept my distance.

Owen talked to me constantly about the fellowship, and sometimes he would get on my nerves. It took me a while, but I finally agreed to attend a large, regional revival meeting that was being held in Maseno. It was to be the first major gathering of the fellowship in the Nyanza region. I was very guarded and still a bit skeptical when I went to the meeting, but God used that occasion to break down some walls that I had built in my life. I began a new journey of fellowship and communion with other believers.

The "Tukutendereza" Fellowship

The Revival, or *Tukutendereza* Fellowship as it came to be known, was a non-denominational phenomenon that confounded the Christian establishment, the latter of which was largely run by foreign mission organizations. I cannot say for sure what really gave rise to this revival, but I understand that the fellowship started in Rwanda around 1933, when I was only about eight years old. By the time I was coming to know Christ in my early 20s, it had spread throughout the region and gained a following of thousands of African Christians in East Africa.

The Gospel of Christ had been brought to East Africa through various, divergent denominational filters that created doctrinal enclaves around the country. The Church Mission Society (CMS) began their work in Western Kenya, Rift Valley, Central Kenya and the Coastal Province. The Church of Scotland Mission and the Methodist Church settled in Central Kenya. The Quakers, the Church of God and PAOC worked mostly among the Luhya community in Western Kenya.

Africa inland Mission (AIC) focused on the Rift Valley and parts of Nyanza Province, while the Seventh Day Adventist Mission (SDA) and the Lutheran Mission concentrated their work in Kisii and South

Nyanza. At that time, only the Catholic Church had established itself all over Kenya.

The Tukutendereza Fellowship cut across all these boundaries. The Fellowship was somewhat of a rebellion against the Christian establishment in the region. It was a youthful movement that grew out of a deep-seated conviction that the church was becoming a pious, ritualistic organization that no longer preached repentance from sin and life-changing salvation. Those in the movement believed that salvation needed to be demonstrated visibly in one's lifestyle and choices. Who would have thought that the "natives" to whom foreign missionaries had brought the Gospel would one day rise up to defend the Gospel against being diluted by those very missionaries?

The Fellowship was vocal about issues of immorality and traditional practices that they deemed to be not in keeping with Scripture. As it grew in strength and numbers, it caught the attention of not only the church community, but also of the colonial administration. The administration feared that a movement of this type could transform into a political movement that could threaten social order. However, the attitude of the Revival was decisively to shun politics.

In spite of its being initially portrayed as a radical "sect" by many established Christian bodies, the Revival did not become a sectarian movement outside the church. Instead, it grew in the church – defying denominational, ethnic and national boundaries. Despite their strong and passionate criticism of the church, members of the movement have always seen themselves as called to witness to the church from within the church.

Growing In My Faith

When I joined the East Africa Revival Fellowship, there was a small celebration in the local community. Apparently, it was deemed as a significant affirmation that the Principal of Nyang'ori Junior School had joined the movement. Some brethren came over to see me and to encourage me to be strong in my new-found faith.

The brethren informed me that the spiritual walk was not going to be easy, and I should be prepared to let go of anything that had become part of me that was not godly. They urged me to confess to God any sins that I had committed against Him; to put things right with the people I had offended; and to return or replace any item that I might have acquired from anybody wrongly.

I listened carefully with an open mind and allowed myself to hear through them what God was saying to me. I was very conscious of the many wrongs in my life, and I didn't know where to begin. I had done very many bad things prior to my healing and salvation.

At that moment, my mind drifted to something over which I had been feeling a sense of guilt. It had to do with taxes which I should have been paying but had been evading by telling lies.

The school at which I was employed was located between two districts: Kakamega and Kisumu. There was a requirement at that time for every employed person to pay a local tax to the Local Native Council (LNC) at the District Headquarters. In my case, whenever I went to Kakamega and was asked if I had paid my LNC rates, I would say "Yes, I have paid them in Kisumu." Whenever the question came up in Kisumu, I would say that I had paid in Kakamega. I had gotten away with this for quite some time, and now as I prayed with the brethren, I realized that this was actually theft.

I asked the brethren for advice. They told me to go to the District Commissioners of both districts and confess that I had been cheating them. Given my senior position, it was not an easy thing to do. I risked the possibility of being fined heavily or even jailed. I also faced the risk of damaging my reputation in the eyes of the missionaries, students and other people who regarded me with respect. Yet, I decided that it was the right thing to do, and I trusted that God would honor my obedience.

After praying about it, I reported myself to the two District Commissioners. I informed them that I had lied and stolen money from them. In both places, I was interrogated and eventually forgiven. I was given a clean slate and warned against repeating the offence.

Another wrongdoing that the Lord brought to my mind was gossip. Over the years, I had spoken ill of many of the missionaries. The Lord impressed upon me that I needed to repent of that sin. I asked God to forgive me – and then the brethren encouraged me to go to those that I could find and ask them for their forgiveness. This was also not an easy thing to do, but I felt such freedom when I had done it. I also asked for forgiveness from some of the teachers and even students that I had mistreated. Some of them were shocked at the change that came over me. This was not the Richard that they had known.

As we prayed together with the Revival brethren, God revealed other things to me. For example, I had taken some school books to my own library and had claimed that they were mine. I decided to take them back to the school openly and confess that it had been my intention to keep them.

With these daring steps, my Christian journey had begun in earnest. There were many other areas of my life that God would have to deal with, and even now He continues to work in me to make me more like Christ.

I am still a member of the East Africa Revival Fellowship and even though the numbers have dwindled over the years, we still meet regularly to fellowship and strengthen each other. Like in any gathering, there are differences in view points and beliefs within the Fellowship. But we are held together by a common love for Jesus. Some people in the Fellowship believe that one is not saved if they are not part of the Fellowship. I have never subscribed to such extremist views. I believe that God is at work in the lives of Christians everywhere, and that He is no respecter of persons.

In my own life, I can testify that God has used simple people with whom I fellowship to challenge me, to shape me and to encourage me in my walk as a Christian. Early in my journey, I learned how important it is for a Christian to read the Bible daily. I did this whenever I found the opportunity, and God spoke with me through this Book. I have read it from cover to cover countless times, and I still am amazed at just how much I still have to learn. I also learned early on to pray daily. Jesus is my very close friend, and I set aside time every day just to talk with Him.

I have learned to appreciate the local church as a gathering of God's people, and I do not know how anyone can grow in Christ if they do not belong to a local church. Above all, I have learned to value the relationships of fellowship and accountability that I have with brothers and sisters in Christ. Scriptures tell us in Hebrews 13:16 "But do not forget to do good and to share, for with such sacrifices God is well pleased."

CHAPTER 5

FOCUS ON THE FAMILY

*Behold, children are a heritage from the Lord, the fruit of the
womb a reward. Like arrows in the hand of a warrior are the
children of one's youth. Blessed is the man who fills his quiver
with them! He shall not be put to shame when he speaks with
his enemies in the gate*

Psalms 127: 3-5

On Saturday, January 5, 1957, I stood in front of Rev. Jack Lynn, a PAOC missionary, and recited my marriage vows to my new bride, Dinah Auma. It was the beginning of a new journey with a woman who has since then given me eight wonderful children and has stood by me for better or for worse for the past 58 years.

If there is one area of my life where I have seen God's grace, it is in the journey of maintaining a marriage and raising children. My wife, Dinah, and I have experienced all the joys and pains of parenthood and, looking back, I can only thank God for His grace and faithfulness to His own Word.

By today's standards, I got married quite late in my life. I was 32 years old, and my young bride was only 18. I can't help chuckling to myself when I consider the paradox of how upset I become now when I hear of a young, teenage girl quitting school to start a family. If I were given a chance to go back and relive my life, I probably would encourage Dinah not to think about marriage at such a young age and to concentrate on her studies instead. But that, of course, is wishful thinking. God does not grant us the privilege of going back to relive our lives.

Life is real, and it presents us with choices that are irreversible. Our choices have consequences – sometimes good and sometimes not so good. The choices we make also come with responsibilities. This is especially true in the area of relationships between men and women.

I believe that marriage is a solemn covenant that must be protected at all costs. Marriage was God's idea, and I believe strongly that His plan was for a man and his wife to raise a family together and to pass on to their children the inherent value of a father and mother staying together. Unfortunately, as the years have gone by, I have seen the rate of divorce increasing. While I do not have the right to pass judgment, I am saddened by the ease with which young people seem to walk in and out of marriage today.

When I gave my vows to my wife on that warm Saturday morning in1957, my mindset was that we would stay together until death would separate us. It is a covenant that I have clung to throughout our marriage, even when things became very difficult.

A Conflict of Priorities

Six years into our marriage, in 1963, a door opened for me to go to the United States for further studies. Under normal circumstances, this should have been a moment of elation. Yet I found myself struggling to know how to find a balance between two very important priorities: my family and my career.

At that point in my life, we had four young children and a fifth one on the way. The oldest child, our daughter Rhoda, was just turning six years old and would be starting school in the next school year. I knew very well that if I chose to take up the overseas study opportunity, the child that Dinah was carrying would be born in my absence, and I would not be able to see him or her for several years.

To go or not to go was the choice before me. I was only too aware of the importance of those early years in the development of children, and I wondered if I would live to regret having missed out on those crucial times of their development as well as on our life together as a family.

It was not an easy decision, but in the end, I decided to take the opportunity and travel to the States. In those days there was no email, and the cost of telephone communication was prohibitive. For three good years, I was virtually cut off and disengaged from my wife and children.

In sharing this story, I cannot categorically say that a family should always be physically together. There are many people, including civil servants, evangelists, soldiers and others whose jobs often require them to be in places where they cannot be with their families. All I can say is that this comes at a cost. The time and distance between me and my wife for the three years in which I was away definitely hurt our marriage. It allowed for a gap to develop between us that would take many years to close.

I attained my Bachelors degree in the United States in three years. In August 1966, I returned to Kenya to take up a job that, from what I could see, was going to be very demanding on my time. It was a leadership job as Secretary General of the Christian Churches Education Association (CCEA). I will come back to the significance of this posting later, including the fact that I was the first African in this position.

I was almost forty years old when I returned from the United States, and I felt some pressure to settle down quickly and to establish myself as a professional. The study leave had opened my eyes to the wider world, and I was very conscious of just how few Africans in the "system" at that time had the privilege of going overseas to study. I had majored in history, but the specific course of study really didn't matter very much given the small number of people who had university degrees.

When I landed in Nairobi, before I even went to Kisumu to see my family, I was invited to spend a day with Rev. Ronald Dain, the outgoing Secretary General of CCEA. I spent an awkward night at his home where we talked a lot about the job ahead of me. I began to sense a racial superiority complex that I had grown to abhor, even before I left for the United States.

Rev. Dain wanted me to start the job immediately, but I said that I would need a month to reconnect with my family. I would need time to settle them in Nairobi, where I would be stationed. This would mean finding a home, finding schools for the children and finding a church that would be our home away from home.

The following morning, I flew to Kisumu to be with my family. I was very nervous. On my arrival at the small Kisumu airport, I was met by a small crowd of people from the Revival Fellowship of which I had become an intricate part before I left the country. My wife and children were lined up on one side staring at me as I made my way toward them. I greeted the brothers and sisters who had broken out in that familiar revival song, *Tukutendereza Yesu.*

I finally reached my wife and I hesitated for a moment. The glare of the spotlight was too much, and I must confess I did not know if I should give her a public embrace or merely shake her hand. I extended my hand to her and we shook hands. I then proceeded to pick up each of my children, one by one. Looking back, I realize that I was overly self conscious. I remember wishing that this could have been a more private, family affair.

From the airport, we all proceeded to the home of my now late brother-in-law, Joseph Ogola and his wife Grace. There, I was treated to a welcome feast. It was a long day of fellowship and testimonies, and I sat quietly through most of it, observing my children who were wandering in and out. They had grown so much.

Rhoda, who was nine years old at the time, had joined Thogoto Junior School, a very good Church of Scotland Mission primary school in what is now Kiambu County. My employer, CCEA, had kindly extended a loan to me that had enabled me to put her in that school while I was doing my studies. My sister-in-law, Mary Oburu, who lived in Nairobi, had been her guardian during my absence. Mary's husband, Samuel, had gone to the United States before me, and he was back in the country at the time.

I was particularly struck by my son Paul, whom I had never seen. Dinah had been pregnant with him when I left for the United States. Paul was almost three years old and was a very active child. I was shocked to learn for the first time that he had rickets, a condition that affects bone development in children. It causes the bones to become soft and weak and can lead to bone deformities. Paul's legs were severely bowed, and the little two-year-old looked awkward as he struggled to walk.

I decided that Paul's legs would be one of my priorities in the coming year. By God's grace, we were able to have his legs operated on in Nairobi, and he has since lived a normal life.

Karin was a shy, pretty little girl. She was just a baby when I left, and now she was walking around. I called her to me at one point, but she ran to her mother instead, amidst some laughter from those who were sitting around the room.

Peter kept walking in and out. He would stop and stare at me, and then he would run back outside to play. He was now seven years old and was attending school at Ogada Primary School. He and Mary, his follower, had moved in with their grandmother, who lived in Nyahera, just down the road from the school. Dinah and the younger children were still staying in Nyang'ori, which was some five kilometers away.

God would give us three other children: Jim, Timothy and Phillip to round off the number at eight. Of all the things that I have to be thankful for, first among them is the family that the Lord gave me. Raising these eight children has had its highs and lows, but I can say with confidence that the welfare of my family is the number one responsibility that I have before God.

A Priestly Duty

When I married Dinah, I knew even then as a relatively young Christian that I had been called to be the priest in my home. My reference point is the Bible, which provides a good guideline on the whole subject of priesthood. In the Old Testament, we are shown the things that a priest was expected to do, and I look to these illustrations to help me in my priestly duty as a father.

First of all, a priest in the Old Testament had to keep himself undefiled by sin. Since he had to make sacrifices for the people, he could not be in a place of sin himself. Every time a priest came on duty, the first thing he did was to make atonement for his own sin before being in a position from which he could intercede for the people. If the high priest was harboring sin when he went into the Holy of Holies, he would die.

The first thing that I have to confess is that I am a sinner. I know that God hates sin, and when I walk or dwell in sin, I block the power of God to work in my life and the life of my family. I confess my sins daily to God, and I ask Him to forgive me and cleanse me – not just for my sake, but for the sake of the family for which He holds me responsible as a priest.

The spiritual cover of a father over a family is a serious matter. This is especially true here in Africa where many of us grow up surrounded by pagan traditions and customs that have the potential to spiritually cripple families and even entire communities. As I look back now, I see how God enabled me to navigate the negative cultural traps of my own Luo community.

As I mentioned at the beginning of this book, I was born in a village called Randago in South Alego, one of the administrative locations in what is today called Siaya County, in the western part of Kenya. My family belonged to a clan called Agoro, one of the smallest among several clans into which the local population was divided. Some of the more prominent of these clans were Kanyinek, Kakan and Karuoth.

The environment in which I grew up was steeped in cultural traditions including that of witchcraft, which I consider retrogressive. My maternal uncle was one of the leading sorcerers in our village, and people would go to him to consult him on all manner of issues. To this day, many of the people of Alego are very superstitious, and many live in constant fear of bad omens, spells and curses.

I remember that when I started going to school, my uncle, the witchdoctor, wanted me to carry some of his "magic" that was supposed to help me excel. I declined to do so because leaders in the school and church that I had started going to had told us that these things were useless. Unlike several other children in the village, I was convinced by the stand of the school. I was told more than once that I was going to die if I did not walk around with some protective paraphernalia from the witchdoctor. But by God's own doing, I have outlived all those people who predicted my death.

I have refused again and again to bow to pagan practices in my life, and more so when I became a Christian. I believe that God has protected my family from many ills because I stood in the gap for them and provided priestly cover against the forces of darkness.

I remember, for example, when my father died in 1975. I was then working in Nairobi. The news came to me as I was chairing a meeting at the Limuru Conference Centre. When I received the news, I immediately began to pray. I knew that I was about to head into a major confrontation with members of my community.

Many people in the Luo community practice elaborate rituals when someone dies. Since my father was an elderly man and very prominent in the clan, his burial would need to be conducted in the culturally prescribed way. As his oldest son, there would also be expectations placed on me to adhere to certain traditional practices that, in my view, were contrary to my faith in Christ.

It so happened that, during that period, there was an outbreak of cholera, a deadly, water borne disease that can kill even a healthy adult in a matter of hours. With a very short incubation period, cholera can easily explode into an outbreak, as was the case in Western Kenya at the time. Several people had been confirmed dead from the disease, and the government had issued a directive that dead people would need to be buried immediately in order to help curb the outbreak. It would be necessary my father's funeral to take place very soon.

Before leaving Nairobi for the village, I called the District Commissioner in Siaya and pleaded with him not to have my father buried before I got there. He was a sensitive man, and he urged me to hurry up and come as soon as I possibly could. I was able to arrive at home in time to manage and control the activities surrounding the burial. The ceremony was conducted by the Church of Christ in Africa, where my late father had become a member in his senior years.

Customary tradition demanded that, upon the death of my father, I would shave my head and the heads of my sons. I refused to do this. I also refused to participate in or invest in a feasting frenzy that has become the hallmark of Luo funerals. My father had passed away, and all I wanted to do was to give him a decent, dignified burial and then move on with our lives. I was adamant about not being dragged into unnecessary activities and unnecessary expenditures. Looking back now, I must have come across as crazy to the people of my humble village.

After a burial, tradition demands that members of the immediate family stay up all night sitting around a fire that would normally be kept going for several days. In my ongoing defiance, I resisted this too and took my wife and my children to my small hut to sleep for the night. Our intention was to travel back to Nairobi the following morning. The next day, we rose up early, and I put my wife and children on a bus to Nairobi. I then got into my car and drove off to Eldoret to attend a meeting.

Needless to say, the community was aghast at my behavior. What they and, unfortunately, many Christians also do not understand, is that a person cannot live in two different worlds. The Kingdom of God is opposed to the kingdom of darkness. I was prepared to be cast out by my family and community rather than to be cast out by God.

The main point I want to make here is that being the priest of the home is an awesome responsibility, and any man entering into the covenant of marriage must understand that God takes priesthood seriously. Fortunately for us, Jesus has made the one and only sacrifice for sin on our behalf. We no longer have to slaughter animals in order to bring their blood before the altar of God. All we have to do is to repent and ask for forgiveness, which is already provided. Our children need to see us as willing vessels, quick to repent and quick to ask for God's forgiveness. It is only through our example that they will learn to turn to God instead of running away from Him.

At a very practical level, I made a point of gathering my family at least several times a week to read the Bible, sing some songs and pray together. We would usually begin our devotional time with singing. I am not much of a singer myself, but my wife and children all seem to have been gifted with music in their blood.

Through that experience, a few choruses became family favourites – or maybe I should say that they became my favourites. There are two in particular that we still sing whenever we are together as a family. These two are

1. "Thy loving kindness is better than life" (Psalms 63:3)

2. "I will sing of the mercies of the LORD forever." (Psalm 89:1)

The family devotion time became a very special time for me. Perhaps more than anything else, it became for me a time to connect with my family. We shared a lot during that time, and I was able to learn about many things that were going on in the lives of my children even as they were growing up and becoming more and more independent. The devotion time also gave me a chance to establish some semblance of a family tradition that I hoped my children would carry into their own families.

Finding My Place in the System

Going back to the challenges of my return to Kenya after my three-year study leave, I can confirm that the time in the United States had changed me in many ways. It had made me more independent and perhaps a bit more ambitious and driven than I was when I left Kenya. On the other hand, the experience of being away had also reinforced certain traits in my personality that would continue to set me apart as a unique individual in the various places where God would call me to serve over the next four decades.

I started this new season of my life with a lot of enthusiasm. There were so many loose ends that I would have to pull together. The next four weeks would be one of the most intense periods of my life.

At some point during those four weeks, I travelled to Nairobi to look for a house. Mr. Nelson Kivuti, who was then holding the CCEA Secretary General position in an acting capacity, took me to a house that had been secured for me in Nairobi's Eastleigh area.

When we got to the house, I asked Nelson why I was being given this house in this low income part of Nairobi, and yet my predecessor, Rev. Dain, had been living in the up-market suburb of Milimani in the western side of the city. Nelson looked at me blankly, understanding the essence of my question but perhaps not wanting to be drawn into the implications of that particular conversation.

The truth was that there were two standards that had been set: one for Europeans and another for Africans. I fought to suppress my anger at the blatant racism that I had naively thought would have become less blatant with independence. I had experienced racial discrimination in the United States, but I was not about to tolerate it in my own country.

Ultimately, I refused to take the house that Nelson had shown me. That afternoon, I went to see Archbishop Beecher, the CCEA Chairman. I told him flatly that I would not accept the house that I had been shown and asked him why it was difficult to get me a house on the west side of Nairobi where he and other Europeans were living. It was an uncomfortable conversation, and his initial response was that I should not be prideful. We continued to argue, and it was clear that my stand was going to become a major issue between me and the organization, even before I started the job. In the end, I was given a house in Lavington, a suburb in the west side of Nairobi.

As the August school holidays came to an end, Rhoda needed to return to school. I decided to drive back to Kisumu to pick her up and to settle her in school before I would return to collect the rest of the family. I would still need to look for a school in Nairobi for Peter and Mary, but that could wait a bit.

I did the necessary shopping for Rhoda and eventually took her back to school. I then returned to Kisumu to pick up the rest of the family. Given the location where we were now going to live, the nearest school for our other children would be Lavington Primary School, a predominantly European school.

Going to Lavington Primary was quite a cultural adjustment for Peter and Mary who had started their schooling in a rural school with mud structures for classrooms. I recall Mary asking me when I came to pick them up at the end of the first day in school, "Baba, what were they saying?" I smiled and told her that I did not know because I was not there to hear their words.

In September 1966, I moved into my Church House office, located in the Central Business District (CBD) of Nairobi, and began a new season of life. In many ways, I was entering a new world that was opening up before me.

But most importantly, being settled in Nairobi meant that we were family again. Dinah would later get a secretarial job at one of the leading banks in the city, and we would eventually adjust to a new urban lifestyle that would frame our existence for the next forty or so years.

CHAPTER 6

MORE THAN JUST A CHURCH

For as we have many members in one body, but all the members do not have the same function, so we, being many, are one body in Christ, and individually members of one another. Having then gifts differing according to the grace that is given to us, let us use them: if prophecy, let us prophesy in proportion to our faith; or ministry, let us use it in our ministering; he who teaches, in teaching.

Romans 12:4-7

Looking back over my life, I can see one area of my life in which I was able to utilize virtually all my gifts, and in which the Lord enabled me to make a significant contribution. It was also an area in which He also graciously allowed me the joy of seeing the fruits of my labour. I am speaking here of my involvement and contribution toward building what is today known as Christ is the Answer Ministries (CITAM). With great joy, I can say that CITAM is one of the most respected and best governed churches in all of East Africa.

The Lord led us to join this congregation at a time when it had less than 200 members. Together with a band of God's faithful servants, we laid the foundations – spiritual, legal, administrative and relational frameworks that have enabled the church to grow into a successful, multi-faceted, multi-branch and multinational organization with well over 40,000 members.

During my time with the church, CITAM went through many significant transitions. The most significant of these transitions, in my opinion, was the transition from a missionary-run organization to a fully Kenyan church with its own constitution and governance structures that have made it a role model for many other church organizations.

I remember in 1996 when Rev. Dennis White handed over leadership of the church to Rev. Boniface Adoyo and ushered in a new season in which the church would be run by Kenyans instead of by missionaries from Canada. To the glory of God, CITAM has continued to grow from strength to strength, and its impact is being felt around the world.

In this chapter, I want to share a few recollections that stand out to me as I glance backward and reflect on our journey with the church. I want to repeat that my purpose for sharing this testimony is not to boast, but to give God glory. I want to encourage those who are in the journey and those who will follow to devote themselves to building the Kingdom of our Lord. As the Apostle Paul says in *1 Corinthians 3:8, "The one who plants and the one who waters have one purpose, and they will each be rewarded according to their own labour".*

Our Search for a Home Church

One of the things that I had purposed to do when I brought my family to Nairobi was to find a church that I would be able to call our home church. From the exposure I had gained during my brief period in the United States, an important criterion that I had set in my search for a home church was that I wanted a church that was child-friendly. I wanted a church in which my children would be involved and effectively be taught the word of God.

During our first few weeks in Nairobi, we took time to visit different churches. Although I still considered myself an Anglican, I was not particular about the denomination that we would choose. I just wanted a good church where we could settle and find a home.

The first obvious place for me to start was Lavington United Church, which was just a few kilometers away from where we lived. I will not say too much, only that I remember how we just did not feel welcome there. Thereafter I tried all the major churches in Nairobi. All Saints' Cathedral at the time was a very stiff, upper class congregation where my children could not have felt at ease.

From there, we went to the Nairobi Baptist Church. I really loved the preaching there, but again, there was no organized Sunday school where our children would hear God's Word. So we decided to try St. Andrews Church. There we found for the first time an organized Sunday school, but after the service, we felt completely left out because virtually everyone was speaking in Kikuyu, a language which we did not understand.

At some point during this period, I met Rev. John McBride, a PAOC missionary who was leading a small fellowship that PAOC had started to reach out to the urban population in Nairobi. Rev. McBride and his wife Ella had taken over leadership of the fellowship a decade or so earlier from Rev. Richard and Olive Bombay. Rev. Bombay was the founding Pastor of the church.

Pastor McBride was not a stranger to me. He had been my Principal and teacher at the Nyang'ori Junior Secondary School that I had attended as a teenager. He invited me to bring my family to the next Sunday service. It was a truly enjoyable experience, and I knew in my heart that we had found our home church. Pastor McBride was very warm and welcoming, and he encouraged me to work with him in building the church into what we wanted it to be, as opposed to looking for the perfect church. I accepted the challenge and appreciated the warm welcome that we received.

Dinah and I got involved in different ministries including Sunday school, ushering, women and men ministries and others. There were simply not enough hands for the work that needed to be done, and I decided that I would plough myself into this ministry.

The official name of the Church at the time was Pentecostal Evangelistic Centre (PEC). However, it was already widely known as the Valley Road Church or the Christ is the Answer Church because of the prominent "Christ is the Answer" sign that hung over the church fence onto the busy Valley Road. Many years later, during the tenure of Pastor Mervin Thomas, the name of the church would be changed to Nairobi Pentecostal Church. It would be changed again in the late 1990s to Christ is the Answer Ministries (CITAM).

Against the Grain

My decision to become part of a Pentecostal church raised eyebrows among many of my colleagues and associates in the ecumenical circles in which I worked. My employer, CCEA, was itself an ecumenical organization affiliated with the National Council of Churches of Kenya (NCCK), an umbrella body that would later directly employ me for some 22 years.

I was aware that I was making a statement about my independence and perhaps even about my non-conformist approach to decision making. Neither NPC nor Pentecostal Assemblies of God (PAG), the local partner of PAOC, were members of the National Council of Churches of Kenya (NCCK), the umbrella body for mainstream evangelical churches.

It seemed odd to many of my contemporaries that I would choose to join a charismatic Pentecostal church. The leadership of the Anglican, Methodist, Presbyterian and Lutheran churches – all of whom belonged to NCCK – generally viewed the Pentecostal movement negatively. Why would Richard Ondeng, a conservative member of the Anglican Church, decide to become part of the Valley Road Church? This was the question in the minds of many of my professional peers.

But I had made up my mind, and I knew that my family and I were where the Lord wanted us to be. At the time of joining the church, I was peripherally conscious of the preparation for this new encounter that the Lord had put me through right from childhood. In chapter two, I narrated how I first came into contact with PAOC missionaries, and how much my life had been impacted through them. Looking back today, I smile as I see God's guiding hand, and how He not only led me to the Nairobi Pentecostal Church, but enabled me to play a significant role in its development.

Seasons of Growth

Pastor McBride was an excellent Bible teacher. He was a patient, down-to-earth man with the heart of a shepherd. He and Ella left Nairobi in 1968 and were succeeded by Rev. and Mrs. Eugene and Lois Johnson. Rev. Johnson served as transitional Pastor for about two years before handing over to Rev. Mervyn Thomas. Rev. Thomas, a Welsh minister, led the church from 1970 to 1983. He and his wife Sheila had ministered in the U.K. before coming to Africa as missionaries where they spent a total of 25 years, first in Tanzania, before taking up the leadership of the Pentecostal Evangelistic Centre.

A number of significant transitions took place under the leadership of Pastor Thomas. First, the name of the church was officially changed from Pentecostal Evangelistic Centre to Nairobi Pentecostal Church (NPC). Secondly, NPC became a prominent landmark in Nairobi as the congregation grew and the ministries of the church expanded to cater to the diverse segments of the Nairobi population. It continued to grow until we could no longer fit into the sanctuary, and the Sunday morning services spilled out into the parking lot. The Board of Deacons, on which I was serving as Secretary, responded to this challenge by approving plans to break out the side walls in order to expand the seating capacity of the church.

One evening, as I was walking through the church building, it struck me that we had invested so much in facilities for children, and that these facilities were only being used on Sunday mornings. It seemed shameful to me that we were not making use of the classrooms during the other six days of the week.

That same week, I put a proposal to the Deacon Board suggesting that NPC should start a kindergarten. The Board deliberated on the idea and, in the end, it was approved. NPC Kindergarten opened its doors to the members of the church. With that move, the church began a new journey into the realm of education. Some years later, the leadership would eventually accede to pressure from the same congregation to start a primary school.

NPC's education program has since grown into an integral part of its ministry to the people of Nairobi. That journey has had its own ups and downs and struggles, but I believe that the Lord continues to bless the church as it seeks to be a holistic ministry, ministering to the spirit, body and mind.

As the numbers continued to swell, it became evident that we would eventually have to move the church to another location. That location ended up being the plot next door to where the church was located. On that plot was a hotel called Hotel Roma. The church approached the owner of the hotel to see if he would consider selling the property to the church, but he would hear nothing of it.

The elders and deacons took time out to pray over the matter, and the Lord intervened. Through the influence of Pastor Thomas and others on the Deacon Board, a mediation process was initiated that resulted in the owner selling the property to NPC. After acquiring the property, the church immediately embarked on plans to construct a new church building. Drawings for the new sanctuary were done by Stan Webb, an African American architect who was then also a member of the Deacon Board.

Pastor Thomas retired in 1983, just when the church was beginning construction of the new sanctuary. Rev. Roy Upton, a gifted evangelist, took the helm of leadership and saw the church complete construction of the new building. Between 1983 and 1987, Rev. Upton built on the foundation laid by his predecessors and enabled the church to experience immense growth and harvest.

I continued to serve on the Deacon Board during Rev. Upton's term of service. As he wound up his ministry in Nairobi, we requested PAOC to help us identify a successor. Under the constitution of the church, pastors were to be hired by the Deacon Board, but this was done in a spirit of collaboration with PAOC.

As the Lord would have it, I would remain on the Church Board throughout the tenure of Rev. Denis White, a powerful charismatic leader who succeeded Pastor Upton in 1987. Pastor White and his wife, Esther, left indelible marks on NPC. The effects of their ministry continue to be felt up to now. NPC grew exponentially under their leadership, leading to some significant decisions that would effectively overhaul the governance structure of the church.

During Pastor White's tenure, the church began to recruit young local pastors who were to be groomed and mentored by Pastor White for leadership. He was very intentional and vocal about how he was going to bring an end to the era of PAOC missionaries being sent all the way from Canada over to Kenya to lead the church.

Pastor White's strong personality, disciplined lifestyle and gift for teaching attracted a lot of attention to NPC and made the church very influential, even in the nation's political sphere. President Moi came to the church so frequently that many people began to refer to NPC as "President Moi's church". In spite of all this attention, the White's remained focused on building the structures of the various ministries. Of particular note are the women's and children's ministries, the Kiserian street children program and the prayer meetings, all of which were directly coordinated by Sister Esther White.

True to his promise, Pastor White stepped down dramatically in 1997 and handed over leadership of the church to Rev. Boniface Adoyo. The White's moved out of the Senior Pastor's house on the Valley Road compound and moved into an apartment in Karen where they would lead the process of establishing the new NPC Karen assembly.

Pastor Adoyo had served under both Rev. Upton and Rev. White. By the time he took over leadership of NPC, I had stepped down from being a Deacon, but continued to serve as an elder in the church.

Pastor Adoyo's elevation to the newly created position of Bishop was not an easy process. There were skeptics, both among missionaries and members of the NPC congregation, who questioned whether or not he would be up to the task. As it turned out, NPC continued to grow, and under his leadership, the church expanded the number of branch assemblies in different parts of the country. NPC was now no longer a Nairobi-focused church, but instead was already moving toward what would later become a global ministry. The church was then renamed Christ is the Answer Ministries (CITAM).

Pastor Adoyo would complete a successful ten-year stint as Bishop before handing over to Rev. David Oginde. Bishop Oginde, who had worked for many years with the Fellowship of Christian Unions (FOCUS), had come into the church as an administrator under Pastor White. He had moved into pulpit ministry and eventually became Senior Pastor of the Karen assembly that Pastor White had planted before he and Esther wound up their ministry in Kenya.

The PAG Dilemma

My many years of ministry at NPC were not without their difficult moments. Being a leader sometimes calls for making tough decisions that have the potential to bruise relationships. Whether in a church, a work environment or a family setting, a leader who cannot stand firm on matters of principle does not deserve to be called a leader. I would also like to add that a leader does not need to have a title in order to lead.

As I will discuss in a later chapter, one of the most important qualities of leadership is the ability to serve without seeking to be recognized. In *Matthew 6:1, Jesus speaks about this principle and says, "Be careful not to practice your righteousness in front of others to be seen by them. If you do, you will have no reward from your Father in heaven".*

I want to highlight just a few tough issues that we had to navigate, and which I found myself thrust into due to my position of leadership. One of those issues was the uncomfortable and sometimes even hostile relationship that developed between PAOC and the Pentecostal Assemblies of God in East Africa (PAG).

As I mentioned earlier, PAG is a local church organization that was initiated by a PAOC missionary, Otto Keller. Over time, the church was able to stand on its own feet and ultimately became the official local partner of PAOC. With its headquarters in Nyang'ori, PAG expanded mostly in Western Kenya but also had some churches in other parts of Kenya, principally in Kisii and the Rift Valley.

The official partnership between the two organizations lasted over many years, although as the years progressed, the relationship slowly became more of a donor-recipient relationship in which PAG became increasingly dependent on PAOC for financial support. Within the partnership agreement between the two bodies, there was an understanding that neither party would take any major decision without consulting the other.

PAOC had, for the most part, honoured this agreement and had consulted with the leadership of PAG on most major issues related to the various PAOC managed initiatives. These initiatives included the Pentecostal Bible College, the Evangel Publishing House and Pan African Christian College (which later became Pan African Christian University).

Consistent with this practice, PAOC had consulted with PAG on its decision to establish a church in Nairobi. It was a delicate conversation because it was the first church that PAOC would be planting directly, not through or with PAG.

In the early '70s, some cracks began to show in the long standing relationship between PAOC and PAG. Although I was neither a member of PAG nor of PAOC, I found myself thrust in the middle of a number of disputes that would push me to take decisions that would have far-reaching implications for the two bodies.

The first notable issue arose from my own questioning of why PAOC had chosen to establish NPC as a bilingual church. The answer I was given was that, in starting NPC, PAOC's intention had been to raise up an English speaking, urban ministry that would not be under the governance of PAG. Sometime after the church had been started, however, PAG had raised a concern that PAOC had breached its commitment to consult before taking any major decisions.

The PAG leadership had gone further to state that the new church must be conducted in both Kiswahili and English. PAOC had conceded to this demand, and at the time we joined the church, Sunday morning services were conducted with translations from English to Kiswahili and vice versa.

I took it upon myself to raise this issue at the NPC Board of Deacons meeting where an animated discussion took place on the challenges that NPC would face in the future if the decisions of its leaders would always be subject to the endorsement of both PAOC and PAG. It was a difficult meeting that ended in a decision that was bound to create an even bigger rift in the already strained relationship between the two organizations.

By consensus, it fell upon me to go and inform the leadership of PAG that the NPC Board had made a decision to revert to the original plan of having the church become an English speaking assembly. Needless to say, the decision was not well received.

One of the implications of the decision was that PAG would now become very uncooperative on virtually all major issues where their cooperation was requested. For example, a situation arose in which the church had an opportunity to buy a neighbouring house that was for sale, and which the Board felt would make an ideal home for the Pastor.

Following a Board resolution, I went to the bank to see if we could get a loan to purchase the property. The bank agreed to the request, and I proceeded to fill in the necessary application forms. At the bottom of the form line on which the head of the church would sign. I consulted Pastor Thomas on the matter, and he agreed that it would be proper for the General Superintendent and General Secretary of PAG to sign the loan forms.

Without any hesitation, I organized myself and, the next day, I drove to Nyang'ori to see the leaders of PAG. When I reached Nyang'ori, I was told in no uncertain terms that the PAG leadership would not sign any documents and would not provide any support unless the NPC Board reversed their stand on the language issue. I was taken aback, and I returned to Nairobi a bit dejected and frustrated. I realized without a doubt that some major decisions were ahead of us.

An urgent meeting of the NPC Board of Deacons was convened. At that meeting, I explained to them the dilemma that we faced. On the issue of the house, it was clear that we would not be able to get a bank loan without the required signatures of PAG. At the same time, the members were resolute in the view that they would not be manipulated or held hostage by PAG.

In the end, two major decisions were made: a) that the church would approach PAOC for a loan to buy the house for the Pastor, and b) that a formal process would be initiated to give NPC an independent status – distinct from PAOC – and thereby effectively delink the church from the cooperative agreement between PAOC and PAG.

There were many challenges that we would yet have to overcome, but in the end PAOC did come up with the funds needed to buy the house. NPC entered into a formal loan agreement to repay the funds over a stated period of time, and we did acquire the house.

As for the relationship with PAG, the Lord showed us favor as I provided leadership in a legal process that was deemed necessary, but which we all prayed would not result in broken fellowship. I will not go into a lot of detail here, but a protracted legal and institutional development process resulted in NPC being registered as an autonomous church with its own constitution and governance structure.

For a number of years, the church would continue to be led by PAOC missionaries, but this was technically at the request of the local Deacon Board. Under the new church constitution, the Deacon Board was given its mandate and powers from the Annual General Meeting.

Although it had no obligation to do so, the Deacon Board chose to extend a hand of fellowship to PAG in a number of ways including an annual donation to PAG amounting to ten percent of NPC's income for an entire year. This support continued for a number of years and was eventually phased out by the Deacon Board sometime in the 1990s.

Finding the Right Balance

Looking back on my many years as a leader in CITAM, I am conscious of just how much time I spent at the church, sometimes at the expense of my family. I had a full time day job which had many demands including frequent trips around the country and occasionally overseas. But I had committed myself to the church and would spend many of my evenings working at the church office. In the earlier years, we had no administrative staff, so the pastor relied heavily on me as the church Secretary to carry out the administrative duties including processing payments, bookkeeping and dealing with official correspondence.

As the congregation grew, the demands also grew, and I began to find myself struggling to find a balance between my full time job, my duties at the church and the needs of my family. Of the three responsibilities, it was my family that seemed to be sacrificing the most. I remember struggling to find how these could be brought into a correct balance before it was too late.

I can say now without a doubt that it was God's grace, and His grace alone that saw us through. Life is not a straight line, and sometimes we find ourselves in situations that require wisdom and discernment.

Whether at home or at church or in my work place, I have learned to listen to what the Holy Spirit is saying. In times of uncertainty or conflict, His call to us is always to trust and obey. For, as the song says, "there is no other way to be happy in Jesus."

PHOTOGRAPHS

My friend Zadock Otieno and me at Kagumo Teachers College

My wife Dinah and me at our wedding

A family photo, just before I left for the United States for 3 years of studies

That is me on the right, at a meeting with other International students in Goshen College

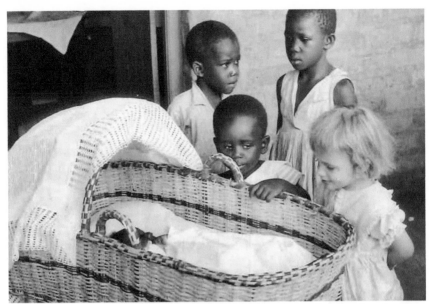

Rhoda, Pete and Mary in 1963 looking at baby Paul in the crib.
They are with a daughter of one of the PAOC missionaries

From left: Mary, Pete, Rhoda (carrying Paul) and Karin (partly hidden)
in Nyang'ori in 1965.

Dinah (holding Karin) with Mary, Pete and Rhoda at a birthday party in Nyang'ori.

Graduation day at Goshen College, Indiana in 1966

My Mother in a 1981 photo in front of her hut in Alego, Siaya District

At NPC with my friend, Bill Cornelius, PAOC Director, and a guest from Canada

With Rev. Mervyn Thomas and officials of Pentecostal World Conference, which was held in Nairobi

*Leading a delegation from NPC to see
H.E. President Daniel Arap Moi at State House*

Introducing my Boss, Dr. Sam Kobia, to the late Dr. Tokunboh Adeyemo

1978 family photo. My wife and children in bell bottoms and afro hair styles

A light moment with my five boys in 1986

CHAPTER 7

LEADING FROM BEHIND

I have been crucified with Christ. It is no longer I who live, but Christ who lives in me. And the life I now live in the flesh I live by faith in the Son of God, who loved me and gave himself for me.

Galatians 2:20

I have many reasons to lift up my hands and praise God as I look back over my 90 years on earth. One of those reasons is the opportunities that God gave me to serve in His Kingdom and to leave some footprints that hopefully others might follow. I say this in all humility because I am very aware of my shortcomings and how much of what I did and achieved was solely by the grace of God and not by my own strength. In that journey of grace, I learned a few lessons about leadership that I want to share.

Let me begin by saying that I am a leader. God called me to leadership, and in that calling, He equipped me and taught me what He expects of a leader. God has a model for effective leadership -- a simple, uncomplicated model that most people do understand, but to which few leaders actually subscribe. That model is called "servant leadership".

Jesus demonstrated servant leadership as he grew and developed the disciples into the leaders of his church. Over the years, I have become more and more convinced that there is no other way to lead effectively than by being a servant. A great leader must first be a servant, and that simple fact is the key to his or her greatness.

In *Mark 10:42-45*, Jesus says, Like many lessons in life, clarity comes only when we look in the rear view mirror. It is when we look behind and reflect on what worked and what did not work that we are often humbled. We are able to see more clearly why God wants us to just trust and obey Him, even when things do not seem to make sense.

My mind goes to one particular season in my life when many people around me expressed that I should have been in front row leadership even though I was, at the time, in a supportive leadership role. This was in 1987 when the long-serving General Secretary of NCCK, Mr. John Kamau, retired, and was replaced by Rev. Sam Kobia.

I have been asked on many occasions if I felt slighted when I was not offered the General Secretary position. From a human perspective, I can understand why people would ask such a question. It would have seemed logical for me to succeed Mr. Kamau after having served as his Deputy for a period of eight years. Yet, I submit that God's ways are not our ways, and His thoughts are not our thoughts. Contrary to conventional thinking, leadership is not about a position. It is about service.

I am convinced that God wanted me to continue in the Deputy position in order to use my experience, networks and organizational skills to undergird and support the organization through a challenging leadership transition. There are a number of critical factors that were at play, and which could have resulted in negative outcomes for both NCCK and for the church in general.

For starters, NCCK had evolved from being a relatively silent association of churches concerned with spiritual and social matters to a highly visible political player that had become a thorn in the flesh to the KANU Government led by President Daniel Arap Moi. This new confrontational posture had earned NCCK the label of being de facto opposition.

There was also uncertainty and perhaps anxiety in many quarters as to how NCCK would evolve post Mr. Kamau, who had been with the Council for nearly three decades and with almost a quarter century as its General Secretary. Leadership change in organizations generally causes fear, and NCCK was not exempted from this pattern. Yet, at the time of Mr. Kamau's retirement, Kenya was embroiled in political agitation, and even within the organization there were political interests that could have tilted the organization in one direction or another, depending on who was leading.

The man who succeeded John, the Rev. Samuel Kobia, was a good friend of mine. He had worked with NCCK in the mid 1970s before leaving the country for study leave. At the conclusion of his studies, he had worked with the World Council of Churches for several years before returning home to join the Council as the director of the Church Development Coordination Programme. Under his leadership, the Council would end up adopting an even higher political profile than before.

Sam Kobia and I became a formidable team and, for the four years that I worked under him, he excelled in the public role for which he had been prepared while I effectively worked behind the scenes, managing internal and external relationships and providing guidance and counsel. More than anything else during that period, God taught me about humility in service. He also opened my eyes to the invaluable qualities of loyalty and trustworthiness. As the political temperature in Kenya rose and NCCK found itself in the eye of the storm, Sam Kobia needed a Deputy who he could trust, and who was not working against him for self interest.

I remember one of the most challenging moments that took place during the early stages of the leadership transition. In 1988, just one year into Sam Kobia's tenure, NCCK came under a barrage of accusations of nepotism, tribalism, mismanagement of assets and mistreatment of staff. It came like a whirlwind, and I found myself right in the middle of the confusion.

With my support, the General Secretary responded to the allegations by initiating an exhaustive investigation to establish the source and credibility of the accusations. I served as the chair of a four-person staff committee that undertook the task of interviewing staff members from all levels and divisions within the Council. At the end of the exercise, we submitted a report to the General Secretary. The process we had undertaken and the report itself brought calm to the situation and exonerated the Council from the criticism, which had found its way into the local media.

Prepared to Serve

My preparation for effective service under two General Secretaries at NCCK began many years earlier, and I don't mind saying that I had more hands-on experience and a greater grasp of the issues in the organization than either of the two men under whom I served. Before going to the United States for my college education, I had been hired by CCEA, then a department within the NCCK (at that time called the Christian Council of Kenya). At that time, education was emerging as the pillar of mission activity in the country, and the mainstream Protestant churches and mission organizations were collaborating in order to find an appropriate and coherent strategy for their work in the sector.

In 1958, the Council decided to register CCEA as a stand-alone organization that would represent the education-related interests of the member churches of CCK. Not long thereafter, I was engaged by CCEA to serve as its Regional Education Secretary, overseeing the education work of the missions and churches in the wider Western Kenya region.

At that time, the church had a significant influence on education in the country, and one of the aims of establishing CCEA was to promote a strong Christian influence in the education and daily lives of youth in Kenya. The best schools in the country, like Alliance High School and Maseno School, were mission-owned schools. Things would change dramatically after independence when, through the new Education Act (1968), the church organizations would cease to be "owners" of the schools and would instead become "sponsors".

The new Education Bill had just been drafted around the time when I was taking over leadership of CCEA upon my return from the United States. CCEA had offered me the job of Secretary General, and I knew that it was an honor to serve as the first African in that position. I also knew that I was walking into a delicate situation that would require very strong leadership and negotiation skills. Part of the challenge, I realized, would involve trying to change the somewhat retrogressive mindsets of the European education officers in the various mission organizations that were still out of step with the realities of the newly independent Kenya.

I took time to visit every mission station around the country, and I spent time with each member church to build relationships and to let them know some of the things that I intended to do as the new Secretary General. I was conscious of the fact that I would experience some resistance, but that was not going to deter me from carrying out the mandate I had been given. From a philosophical standpoint, I was advancing the thought that education in independent Kenya should begin to deal with African issues from an African perspective, and not merely transfer over to Africans the Western values and approaches.

It was during that time that the Kenya National Union of Teachers (KNUT) won a long-standing battle for the creation of a government body, the Teachers' Service Commission (TSC), which would become the formal employer of all teachers in Kenya. The drive by KNUT had been motivated by a desire to see the harmonization of working conditions of teachers across the country. The creation of the TSC meant that the churches would effectively lose control of the teachers working in their schools.

This was a significant change for many reasons. Up to that point, the church organizations had operated with full authority as the employers of teachers, even though, for years, they had been receiving money from the Government for paying those teachers. As a matter of fact, even my own salary as an employee of CCEA had been paid for with funds from the Government as far back as when I was working for the Council before I went abroad for further studies.

When CCEA offered me the job of Secretary General upon my return from the United States, I was unaware that the Ministry of Education considered me a Government employee who was simply seconded to the CCEA. In my own mind, I was working for the churches and was not under the authority of the Ministry of Education. Almost immediately, tension began to surface between me and certain key officials at the Ministry.

Not long after I settled into my new job, I received a letter from the Ministry instructing me to return to the Ministry with immediate effect. When I inquired what this directive was all about, I was informed that some of the positions I had taken in discussions between the Government and the churches showed that my loyalty had been misplaced, and that I was not properly serving the interests of Government, who was my "employer". The letter from the Government thrust me into a dilemma because, if I refused to go to the Ministry, I would be sacked, and CCEA had informed me that it did not have a budget for paying the salary relative to my position.

I informed the Council that I did not want to go to the Ministry, and that they would need to find money if they wanted to keep me. After some internal consultation, I was offered a package by CCEA which was not as secure as the Government package, but which I accepted. From then on, I became a full employee of CCEA.

The downside of this move for me and my family was that I would be forfeiting my accrued pension from 15 years of service that I had given the Government. It was a price I was prepared to pay in order to do a job that I felt God had called me to do. In later years, I would come to appreciate that when we make a sacrifice for the sake of the Kingdom, God always comes through with an even greater blessing.

Tension with Government

The relationship between me and senior government officials at the Ministry of Education became increasingly tense as the discussion over the new Education Bill wore on. The core contention between the churches and the Government was not so much about TSC taking over employment of the teachers as it was about the need for clarity on the role that the churches would play in the new dispensation. I attended numerous meetings with the Government as a representative of the churches in these discussions. I sought clarification from the Government, but it seemed like no one had given any serious thought to the issues involved.

The churches had invested heavily in their various educational institutions, and they were concerned not just about the loss of control of teachers, but also about the prospects of losing their land and other investments that they had made in these schools.

At the height of this tussle, I took it upon myself to convene a meeting of all church leaders to deliberate on the matter. The meeting mandated me to go to the Minister for Education to plead that the Education Bill be held back from being sent to Parliament until the role of the churches had been clarified. The Minister, Hon. Jeremiah Nyagah, refused to delay the Bill. I felt directly challenged by this hard stance, and I made a decision that I would seek audience with President Jomo Kenyatta.

Getting to the President was not easy, but after a while I actually managed to get an appointment to State House. The President was very gracious, and he listened carefully to the concerns that I presented to him. At the end of our meeting, he directed that the Education Bill be withheld.

Not long after that outcome, a dialogue did take place with the Ministry of Education, and we eventually reached some compromises on the issues that had been troubling the churches. Most importantly, we agreed that, while the Government would take over management of the schools that were previously managed by the churches, the churches would, from then on, be considered "sponsors" of those schools.

Effectively, this would mean that the Government would not take over legal ownership of the schools. It also meant that the churches would still be able to use the physical facilities when schools were not in session and, more importantly, they would be able to have a strong hand in the development of curriculum for Christian Religious Education (CRE). This was a major breakthrough. I felt that the hand of God had steered us to that victory.

My Contribution to CRE

As I stated earlier, the many battles that I fought, and the victories that God gave me during my tenure at the helm of CCEA, prepared me well for the supportive role that I would later play in NCCK as Deputy General Secretary. My successful navigation through the difficult dialogue with Government endeared me to the leadership of the churches and mission organizations working across the country. I traversed the country on numerous missions, meeting with school committees, heads of schools and representatives of NCCK's member churches. At one point, I was on 40 different Boards of Governors of schools across the Republic, facilitated by the Ministry of Education.

The CCEA Secretary General was constitutionally mandated to serve as an advisor to NCCK on all matters related to education and church relationships. Given that at the time education had become the highest priority for most church organizations, I found myself involved in one way or another in virtually all areas of NCCK's work.

I could talk about many things that we did, but if I had to pick one particular achievement that gives me a great sense of satisfaction, it would have to be the successful effort that I led in the development of a curriculum for Christian Religious Education in Kenya. When I became involved in the debate over the role of churches in the new education system, I came to realize that CRE was about to become a non-examinable course.

The reason for this was that the Ministry of Education did not want to deal with numerous curricula from different religious bodies that had their own doctrines and preferences. Now that the government was taking over the management of schools, there would have to be either a single curriculum to be followed by all schools – including all Protestant and Catholic schools – if CRE were to be an examinable subject.

I went to the Government and enquired whether they would allow us to try and come up with a consensus curriculum that would satisfy all the Protestant denominational groups as well as the Catholics. It was a tall order – maybe even impossible. But I was given the nod from the Ministry of Education, and I got to work.

I set out to talk with our Catholic counterparts, and we formed a joint working group to wrestle with the issues involved in compiling an acceptable curriculum. There were many challenges along the way. For example, the Catholics argued that religious education begins from the cradle, and it was not just a school issue. For the Protestants, religious education was seen to begin in primary school. This forced us to negotiate and, in the end, we produced a syllabus that incorporated Early Childhood Development (ECD) and yet was consistent with the teachings of all the sponsoring churches.

When I went back to the Ministry of Education, they were surprised – perhaps even shocked – that we had been able to reach a consensus. The Ministry accepted the curriculum. This was a significant milestone in the history of church cooperation in Kenya. As a matter of fact, I do not know of any other country in the world where the Protestants and Catholics have worked together like this in regard to education.

Through it all, I give God all the glory. Even now, I endeavor to follow Jesus, the perfect example of servant leadership. He submitted his own life to sacrificial service under the will of God, and He sacrificed his life freely out of service for others. I read in Matthew 20:28 that He came to serve even though he was God's son and was more powerful than any other leader in the world. May I be more and more like Him.

CHAPTER 8

EDUCATING THE GIRL CHILD

Then our sons in their youth will be like well-nurtured plants,
and our daughters will be like pillars carved to adorn a palace.

Psalm 144:12

One of the clouds that has hung over Kenya's education sector for years is the systemic discrimination against girls. In spite of some progress that has been made over the years to reduce gender imbalance in education, the problem is still quite evident.

Throughout the country, we see different communities still erecting barriers that hinder education for girls. These barriers stem mostly from cultural values and they include early marriage and childbearing.

Economics also plays a big part. Many families cannot afford to send both sons and daughters to school, and so it is quite common for these families to reason that investing in boys brings greater returns to the family. In other words, educating a boy is more profitable than educating a girl because girls eventually leave their parents when they get married and go to the homes of their husbands.

In this chapter, I want to share three stories that are close to my heart, and which have one thing in common: they speak of my involvement with the issue of girls' education and how I grew into an advocate for educating the girl child.

Richard the 'Headmistress'

In early October of 1960 when I was serving as a District Supervisor of Schools, my boss, the then Provincial Education Officer (PEO), called me into his office and instructed me to go and identify suitable sites for two proposed girls' schools that were in the plans for the following year. One of the schools was to be in Kisii and the other in Homa Bay, South Nyanza.

By the end of that month, I had identified two primary schools that had properties that I considered suitable for secondary schools. These were Kereri Primary School and Ogande Primary School.

I returned to Kisumu and reported this to the PEO. My report was presented to the Regional Education Board, which accepted my recommendations. It was decided that the school in Kisii would be called Kereri Girls Secondary School, and the one in Homa Bay would be called Ogande Girls High School.

Following the meeting, the Provincial Education office made requests to two missionary organizations, PAOC and the Church Mission Society, to take a lead in establishing the two schools respectively. The two mission organizations agreed to the proposal.

The first course of action was for both organizations to identify qualified individuals to be appointed to head the two schools. Two months later, PAOC reported that Ms. June Deacon, a Canadian missionary, would take up the job for Kereri Girls, but she was at the time on leave in Canada and would not be back in Kenya until August. By some strange coincidence, the person selected by the CMS to head Ogande Girls was also away on leave in the U.K.

This situation put the PEO in a dilemma, since the Nyanza Provincial Commissioner had made an irreversible promise to the two communities that the schools would be opened in January 1961. He did not want to break his promise.

After a flurry of meetings, the PEO called me into his office and informed me that I would be sent to start the two schools, pending the return of the two ladies. I couldn't believe my ears. What the PEO was effectively telling me was that I was about to become an acting Headmistress for two different schools. Was this not a demotion? How was I to go from being a Senior District Supervisor of Schools to an Acting Headmistress?

I left the office confused and somewhat annoyed. Part of me wanted to refuse the assignment, but I knew that such an action would result in my being fired. I could not afford to be out of a job at that time. We had two small children, Rhoda (3 years) and Pete (2 years). Besides, my wife was pregnant with our third child who was due to be born in February.

I took some time to pray over the matter with a few brethren from the Revival Fellowship, and in the end I accepted to take up the assignment. With little time left, we began to pack our things for the relocation to Kisii. The move was a difficult one, but with the help of members of the Fellowship, we started on our journey to Kisii where we would move into a house that a PAOC missionary had been asked to vacate for us.

On our way there, it began to rain. All of our furniture including the mattresses, beddings and clothes, which were being transported in an open truck, were soaked. Needless to say, we had a very difficult first night in Kisii.

In spite of all the challenges, I knew that I would have to be active in my assignment as soon as we arrived. It was only one week until schools were scheduled to open. The two schools that I had been assigned to supervise were some 60 kilometers apart, and I would have to rush from one to the other frantically trying to prepare them for the new school year.

After two hard days, I realized that the schools were not going to be ready in time. Under pressure, I made a unilateral decision to postpone the opening date by two weeks. I knew that the PEO would be upset about my decision, but I felt convinced that it was the right thing to do.

On the gazetted opening day, the PEO and two European ladies from the Provincial Education Office in Kisumu came out to witness the opening of the two new girls' schools. I had not communicated to them that I was postponing the opening date, and the three visitors from Kisumu were surprised to find me at Kereri Girls, busy cleaning the place with a small group of workers.

As expected, the PEO was furious that I could take such liberty to postpone the school opening date without permission. He hurled a lot of abuse at me, and in the end, I told him that I was prepared to pack up and leave if that is what he wanted. He had no idea how hard I had worked since I had come to take up the two jobs at the two schools.

Through the intervention of a PAOC missionary, Rev. Gordon W. McQuarrie, I agreed to stay on in the job as Acting Headmistress for the two schools until the end of the second term in August that year. Rev. McQuarrie was a man whom I highly respected, and when my son Pete was born I gave him the middle name, Gordon, after Rev. McQuarrie.

With my temporary assignment secure, I made sure that both schools opened according to the revised schedule. I then jumped into the job with a lot of energy. I would shuttle between the two schools, spending one day in one school and the next day in the other. Interestingly, I found myself enjoying this work more than I ever imagined I would. In the process, something happened to me. God used that experience to develop a soft spot in my spirit for the education of girls. My disposition was undoubtedly influenced in part by the fact that I now had two daughters of my own, Rhoda and Mary; I was determined to give them the very best that I could not only in terms of education, but in every opportunity life had to offer.

At the end of the second term, the two ladies who had been away on leave returned and took over responsibility as heads of the two schools. I was immediately relocated back to the Provincial Education Office. Upon my return, the Lord rewarded me with a big promotion that I had not anticipated. I was offered a position by the CCEA to serve as Regional Education Secretary, covering what is now Nyanza, Western Province and Kericho.

In this position, my job would be to coordinate the educational activities of all Protestant churches in that wide region. I took over the office from Rev. Carl Wagonner, a missionary with Africa World Mission, becoming the first African to hold the position.

This appointment was a major boost to my morale, and I would later look back and realize that we cannot outdo God. We also cannot predict what He has in store for us. What He asks us to do is to humble ourselves and to obey Him without grumbling. I held that position with CCEA for two years and then proceeded on my study leave to the United States.

The Lois Bulley Bursary Fund

When I completed my studies in the United States in 1966, I returned to Kenya and accepted an offer from CCEA, my previous employer, to be the Secretary General of the organization. Once again, I sensed that the Lord was placing me there for certain strategic reasons that I would come to appreciate much later.

One of the many fascinating encounters during my tenure at the helm of CCEA occurred in 1974 when I met a visiting British politician named Agnes Lois Bulley. I received a phone call from my good friend, Robert Ridley, a seasoned British banker whom I had come to appreciate as an advisor on matters related to finance. Robert invited me to join him urgently for lunch at the board room of Motor Mart Exchange, one of the large, listed companies in Kenya at the time. He did not explain the purpose for the meeting, but he told me that it was quite urgent.

Given his stature and our good relationship, I took him seriously, and quickly reorganized myself so that I could attend the lunch meeting. When I walked into the room where we were to meet, I found Robert sitting across the table from a heavy-set English woman with long, dark hair.

"Come on in, Richard, I want to introduce you to Hon. Lois Bulley," Robert said. Ms. Bulley stood up and shook my hand. I went around the table and sat across from her. During that one hour together, I came to learn that Lois Bulley was one of those rare human beings that God brings into our lives in order to teach us more about Himself.

The late Agnes Lois Bulley was an extremely wealthy British political activist and philanthropist who spent much of her life fighting against racism and promoting social justice and equality, especially for women. Born into wealth, she felt that she had no right to the inherited wealth but instead owed a debt to the society which gave it to her.

She joined the Labour Party in the United Kingdom in1930 and won a Parliamentary seat, which she used as platform from which to campaign on social issues such as unemployment, social deprivation and women's and children's rights. Over time, charitable work replaced political activity as her principle commitment.

She travelled widely and was particularly drawn to Africa, from where she believed her family had gained most of its wealth. She often talked about how the prosperity of Liverpool, her home town, was built on the African slave trade. Two African countries that she visited frequently were Kenya and Nigeria.

Our lunch meeting was not long, but it was intense. Lois Bulley looked straight at me and said that she wanted to donate some money to a charitable cause, and Robert Ridley had told her that I was one of the people who she should meet. I was taken aback for a moment, but then my mind cleared up and I was able to engage her effectively.

"If you are asking me to recommend an activity for you to support," I replied, "my recommendation would be to set up some kind of bursary fund for girls in Kenya who want to go to school but are not able to because they lack the money that is needed."

Lois looked at me and, for a moment, I thought she was going to cry. Suddenly, without warning, she stood up and came around the table to where I was sitting. I stood up instinctively, thinking that something was wrong. She walked over to me and gave me a huge hug. I was stunned. I looked over at Robert and he was looking at me with a cheeky smile on his face.

On the basis of that brief conversation, Lois Bulley ended up donating some cash and shares that she had inherited in Motor Mart East Africa Ltd. She entrusted me with the responsibility of creating an appropriate legal mechanism for managing and dispensing the funds that were to be used exclusively to support the education of poor but deserving girls throughout the Republic of Kenya.

Shortly after that meeting, I put together a Bursary Committee comprising mostly of senior clergymen aligned to CCEA. Under my chairmanship, the Committee established a process for reviewing and selecting recipients of the funds. Some years later, the Committee decided to register a Trust that would safeguard the assets of the Fund. I served as Chairman of the Trust for several years but later took up the position of Managing Trustee, a position I hold to this day.

Since then, the Lois Bulley Bursary Fund (LBBF) has given financial support to thousands of needy girls in Kenya. The bursaries are given from earnings realized from investing the endowment that was created by Lois Bulley in the money markets.

If there is one realization that has come to me over the period that I have been involved with the LBBF, it is just how great the needs are in Kenya to enable children from underprivileged families to access quality education. So much more support is needed. I wish there were more people like Hon. Lois Bulley.

Moi Nairobi Girls' School

A third story that relates to my passion for girls' education is that of my 38-year involvement with Moi Nairobi Girls School. When I was appointed to the Board of Governors of this school in 1966, it was known as Nairobi Girls Secondary School. It then had only 160 girls, most of whom came from Nairobi's Eastland's suburb, a generally lower income part of the city.

One of the first issues I raised as Board Chairman was the illogical nature of having a day school on the west side of Nairobi that actually was targeting children from the other side of the city. The distance that the girls had to travel to school was long, and many of the girls struggled to reach school on time. It was also a challenge for them to return to their homes at the end of each school day.

The Board discussed the matter, and we reached a decision that the school should be changed from a day school to a boarding school. With that resolution, I went to the Ministry of Education to discuss the modalities of making the change. To my surprise, the officials at the Ministry turned down our proposal, saying that the school had been planned as a day school, and that the Board was going beyond its mandate by trying to change the nature of the school.

My discussion with the officials was a difficult one. I was told that if I wanted to keep pressing the issue, I would be removed from the Board by the Ministry. I was taken aback by this reaction, and immediately I called a school board meeting. In that meeting, I presented the outcome of my visit to the Ministry of Education.

The Board members were as surprised as I had been at the response of the Ministry. After some deliberation, we agreed unanimously to press on with the issue. The members of the Board were incensed that the Ministry would treat them in this way. The decision was recorded in the minutes, and we determined to find a way to address what was, to us, an obvious need.

A few years passed, and at one Board meeting, the subject came up again. We decided then to organize a harambee to raise funds for the construction of a dormitory. This was a bold move, and we were aware that there would be opposition from the Ministry of Education. We spent some time planning how the fund raising would be conducted, and we set a date for the event. The next challenge was for us to identify a prominent personality to be invited as the Guest of Honor.

We went through several names and finally decided to invite the then Vice President, Hon. Daniel Arap Moi to be our Guest of Honor. As Chairman, the task fell on me to reach out to the Vice President and make the request. I had interacted on a number of occasions with the Vice President, and we had developed a good rapport. I did not know, however, whether he would accept our invitation.

When I reached the Vice President's office, I met an Assistant Minister who had been a student of mine many years earlier. He was also walking into the building to see the Vice President. When we exited the lift on the floor on which the Vice President's office was located, we found the Vice President just stepping out of his VIP lift, which was just across the hall.

Vice president Moi greeted the Assistant Minister and then turned to me. The Assistant Minister introduced me as his former teacher, and Mr. Moi replied that he remembered meeting me before. Together, the three of us entered Mr. Moi's office where I quickly handed him the letter of invitation to the fund raising event. Mr. Moi read the letter and asked me a few questions about our objectives. I explained to him why we wanted to change the girls' school from a day school to a boarding school. He nodded his head and said firmly that he would come to the event.

As a courtesy, the Board had also sent an invitation to the then Minister for Education, Dr. Taita Towett. We were very aware that the steps we were taking were going against the wishes of the Ministry of Education, but we would not be deterred. We were also aware that the Minister was a political rival of Mr. Moi, and that there was the possibility of some politics erupting.

On the day of the fund raising, the Minister telephoned me and told me that the event should be canceled. He told me that if it was not canceled, I would cease to be the Chairman of the Board. I politely informed the Minister that I would not be able to un-invite the Vice President. Only he, the Minister, could do that.

The event did take place, and it was a big success. We were able to raise enough money that day to build a dormitory for 100 girls. From that day on, the Vice President took a personal interest in the school and informed us that, if we used the money well, he would be willing to come back for another fund raising event for a second dormitory.

When the construction of the first dormitory was finished, Mr. Moi accepted our invitation to come and preside over its official opening. On that day, we had an impromptu harambee where he made a substantial donation toward the second dormitory. Before he left the venue, he challenged the Board to start the construction of the second dorm as soon as possible.

By that time, the Ministry of Education had accepted the decision to convert the day school into a boarding school. With the Vice President's continued support, the school gained in prominence and grew into one of the biggest boarding schools in Nairobi with facilities for approximately 800 girls.

When Mr. Moi became President, his interest in the school continued, and he directed that I should remain as Chairman of the school. At the instigation of the Board, the name of the school was changed from Nairobi Girls Secondary School to Moi Nairobi Girls School. By that time, I had developed a close relationship with the President, and this relationship enabled me to reach him quite easily whenever we had a need to do so. I tried not to abuse this privilege, but that access was certainly useful on a number of occasions.

With the President's help, the school was later allocated a fifty acre plot of land for expansion. The allocation of the land annoyed some people who seemed to wonder why such prime property should be "wasted" on a girl's school.

In 2004, I decided that it was time for me to retire from the Board. The Board members with whom I was serving at the time asked me to pick a gift that they should give me for me almost four decades of service to the school. I replied that the gift I wanted them to give me was a perimeter wall around the fifty acres that had been allocated to the school. The issue of land grabbing by well place individuals was becoming rampant in the country, and I was afraid that somebody would one day lay claim to part of the land and create a problem for the school.

The school community, including the parents of the children, agreed to raise funds for the wall. People contributed whatever they could, and eventually a wall was built around the school compound.

I retired from the Board a happy man. In a way, I felt like a father releasing his daughter into the care of another man. Although I had served on numerous other school boards around the country, the journey I travelled with Moi Nairobi Girls School was a special one.

I thank the Lord for what we were able to achieve. I also thank His Excellency, President Moi for the contribution he made, not just to Moi Nairobi Girls' School, but to girls' education in general. May the Lord reward him for this wonderful work.

CHAPTER 9

THE LEAST OF THESE

*And if you give yourself to the hungry and satisfy the desire
of the afflicted, then your light will rise in darkness and your
gloom will become like midday.*

Isaiah 58:10

From very early on in my career as an educationist, I had a burden for disabled children, whom I felt, to a large extent, were not adequately catered for in our education system. There are many barriers even today that people with disabilities in Kenya face in getting a decent education. Disability in this context includes long-term physical, mental, intellectual or sensory impairments.

Generally speaking, children with special needs have low priority even within their families. In Kenya, it is not uncommon to hear that a family has literally abandoned a disabled child. Having a child with disabilities is something viewed as shameful or, at worst, a curse of some sort. Some children end up spending their childhood locked up indoors, not even being allowed to venture out to play.

In my mind, the issue of special education is not just a legal or human rights issue. It is also a spiritual issue that speaks volumes about our understanding of what Christianity is all about.

In the early 1980s, the Lord led me to Ghana where He opened my eyes to a need in the area of special education that could be addressed within my sphere of influence. By God's grace, I was able to lay the foundation for what would later become Kenya's first secondary school for the visually impaired. The new secondary school would end up being established as an extension of a primary school for the blind that already existed in Thika, a small town situated about 50 km northeast of Nairobi.

As it currently stands, the Thika School for the Blind is a mixed boarding school that caters for around 300 children from nursery classes through high school. All of its students are visually impaired in one way or another, and many are completely blind. The school provides amazing opportunities for the children. It sets them up to function in the marketplace and to become productive members of our society.

My Eye-Opening Trip to Ghana

When I travelled to Ghana In 1980, I had just joined NCCK as Deputy General Secretary, but I was also still managing CCEA while we searched for someone to replace me. During that period, NCCK received an invitation from our Ghanaian counterpart, the Ghana Christian Council of Churches, requesting NCCK to send someone to attend their Golden Jubilee celebration. Mr. John Kamau, the NCCK boss, was unable to travel, so I was requested to fly to Accra and represent NCCK at the event.

With the support and encouragement of my host, I extended my stay for one week beyond the celebration in order to gain an opportunity to become acquainted with the work that churches in

Ghana were doing. During that week, I travelled around the country and ministered in several congregations. I also had the chance to visit a number of church-supported projects, including schools and other learning facilities.

One of the schools that I was taken to was a secondary school for the blind. I was completely fascinated with what was being done there, and spent the better part of a day at the school. I was keen to know how the school was being run and what lessons they had learned. My mind was racing as I listened to the testimonies of both the young and older people who had gone through the secondary school, and I wondered to myself why we did not have a similar facility in Kenya.

In my capacity as Secretary General of CCEA, I had served on numerous school boards, and one of these boards was the Salvation Army Primary School for the Blind in Thika. I remembered the many discussions we had as a board about what to do with the blind children who were completing the primary school.

Some of the children would end up being admitted at one of several local high schools, but the majority would drop out of school because there were no secondary schools that had facilities and trained teachers that could absorb them.

I returned to Kenya with a determination to do whatever I could to start a secondary school for the blind like the one I had seen in Ghana. I gave my trip report to the Council's Executive Committee, underscoring the things that had made a strong impression on me. I mentioned, for example, the close working relationship that I noted between the Ghana Council and the country's Head of State. I also reported on the very prominent role that the church in Ghana seemed to play in shaping the country's education sector.

At the end of my report, I made a presentation on my visit to the secondary school for the blind in Ghana, and I concluded with a recommendation that NCCK should take the lead in the creation of a similar school in Kenya.

My report was generally well received, except for the last part: my recommendation that NCCK should start a school for the blind. Most of the Council members present felt that I was being a bit ambitious. The general feeling in the meeting was that we should shelve the idea for the time being. However, I was given the freedom to explore the possibility of establishing such a school with other organizations if I felt so led.

Following that meeting, I decided to take time to visit various NCCK member churches to see if any of them would be interested in spearheading this initiative. Unfortunately, none of the mainstream churches that I spoke to were prepared to take up the challenge at the time. The Salvation Army, which already had a primary school for the blind, also expressed that they were not ready to begin a secondary school for the blind.

I was disturbed by this turn of events, but was also determined not to give up. I let the matter rest for some months, and then decided to go back to the Salvation Army Headquarters to seek the counsel of their leadership on how we could pursue this objective. This time, the leadership of the church agreed to work with me. The main obstacle, they said, was that this would be an expensive venture, and they did not feel that they could raise the required grant funding that would be needed to invest in the project.

I was asked whether I thought I could raise money from my contacts. I pondered on the question and replied that it was worth trying. We ended the meeting with a general agreement that, if I could somehow come up with the funds, the Salvation Army would assume responsibility for managing the school.

I felt encouraged by the meeting and, from there, went to see the then Permanent Secretary for of Education, Mr. Peter Gachathi. Peter was a former student of mine at Kagumo Teachers College, and we knew each other well. I made an impassioned presentation to him and explained that this was a noble venture in which the Government of Kenya should play a key role.

Mr. Gachathi became interested in the matter and informed me that he would give me his support. He advised me to go to the Provincial Education Officer (PEO) in Nyeri to discuss the possibility of establishing the school in Central Province. I didn't ask any questions. I thanked him for his good faith, and immediately starting making plans to go to Nyeri.

Within a short time, I travelled to Nyeri to meet with the PEO. To my surprise, he informed me flatly that he was not in favor of having the school situated in Nyeri. He was busy and gave me little time, and I ended up leaving the office a bit dejected. After a few days, I decided to go back to the PS to inform him of the outcome of my visit to Nyeri.

The PS was visibly upset by the outcome of my visit, and he decided to write a formal letter to the PEO, which he copied to me. In the letter, he instructed the PEO to ensure that I was given all the cooperation and facilitation I needed to establish Kenya's first secondary school for the blind.

On receiving the letter, the PEO called me and apologized for having turned me away. He then invited me to come and meet with the Regional Educational Board (REB) to discuss the matter. The following week, I went back to Nyeri to a warm welcome and very productive meeting with the REB. In the end, the REB approved the proposal, and the project became a reality.

The next day, I went to the Salvation Army Headquarters in Nairobi to give them the good news that the Government was going to finance the establishment of the secondary school. They looked at me in disbelief, but I could see that they were happy and prepared to take up the responsibility as they had promised. The first task would be to find qualified personnel to lay the academic foundation for the school.

With God's help, they were able to find an experienced Canadian missionary who agreed to come and help start the school. Being a missionary, his support was covered by the mission organization, and his services would therefore not cost the school any money.

Word spread about the new school, and various individuals, companies and organizations offered help in different ways. Among the early supporters was Sir Charles Njonjo, the then Attorney General, who donated a bus to the school. Other donors included Goethe Institute, a German cultural institute that provided brail equipment. The American Embassy also pitched in, providing some grant funding.

If there is one achievement in my life that thrills me, and which I know only the Lord could have done, it is this project. I served as Chairman of its Board for the first 12 consecutive years. When I stepped down, I was indeed a happy soul who had seen God's hand of favor over a project that I know has given Him great joy.

CHAPTER 10

A SPECIAL TRIBUTE TO PAOC

*How then will they call on Him in whom they have not
believed? How will they believe in Him whom they have not
heard? And how will they hear without a preacher? How will
they preach unless they are sent? Just as it is written, "How
beautiful are the feet of those who bring good news of good
things!"*

Romans 10:14-15

I have decided to dedicate this last chapter to the Pentecostal
Assemblies of Canada (PAOC) because of the extraordinary impact
that this organization has had on my life journey. Over the decades,
I have had the opportunity to serve with many PAOC missionaries,
and I thank the Lord for all that He has done and continues to do
through this ministry. Perhaps more important than anything else, it
was through the ministry of PAOC that I came to know Jesus as my
Lord and Saviour. I want to share a few things that stand out to me
today as I look back.

I first came into contact with PAOC missionaries during my first
year at the Nyang'ori Junior Secondary School in 1942. I was then

a 16-year-old boy – right in the throes of that delicate age of self-discovery and rebellion; that point of transition between childhood and manhood.

I came to know an amazing German man by the name of Otto Keller. Mr. Keller is the person who is credited for not only having started the PAOC mission station in Nyang'ori, but also the person who spearheaded the establishment of the Pentecostal Assemblies of God in East Africa (PAG), a local church organization that would become the official local partner of PAOC in Kenya.

Mr. Keller was not a clergyman. He was actually a businessman with an impressive track record of business success in Germany. At some point in his journey, he had felt the call to sell his business and come to Africa as an independent missionary. He came to Kenya initially just for a transit stop on his way to Tanganyika, which was his intended destination. It so happened that, at that time, Kenya was experiencing a severe famine, and the colonial administration in Kenya had been seeking help from wherever it could find it. While waiting for his entry permit from the then Government of Tanganyika, Mr. Keller had agreed to take up an assignment to help the Kenyan Colonial Government with some famine relief work in the Kisumu area. Due to complications that arose with the Tanganyika permit, he ended up settling in Kenya.

In 1914, he came into contact with some missionaries from Canada and joined with them under the umbrella of the Pentecostal Assemblies of Canada. Through this association, he was eventually ordained as a minister.

Otto Keller was a gifted linguist, and in time, he had come to know the different tribes in the Kisumu district and even became fluent in several of the local languages and dialects. He was also very entrepreneurial and was keen to use his business experience in the Kingdom work.

With the money that he had realized from the sale of his business in Germany, he purchased a seventy-five acre piece of land in the hills of Kisumu from a man named Claude Miller who had come to Kenya about ten years earlier. For some reason, Miller had fallen into disfavour with the government and had been forced to wind up his affairs and leave the country on a fairly short notice. Otto bought the property from him and, on that property, together with his wife, Marion, started the Nyang'ori mission station.

When I arrived in Nyang'ori in 1942, Otto and Marion were still heading the mission station. For reasons that I could not explain then, the couple took a particular interest in me as a student. Perhaps they saw something in me that they liked. I don't know. What I do know is that Otto took me under his wings, frequently inviting me, along with a few other students, to his home.

Sadly, Otto died a year or so later after nearly 32 years in Africa. He died at the age of 54 from an infection following an appendix operation. He was buried at the Nyang'ori Mission in Kisumu. Marion, his wife, continued with the work until other missionaries came to take over. She then returned to Victoria in British Columbia until her death in 1953.

The Expansion of PAOC Work in East Africa

Over the ensuing years, God enabled PAOC to send more missionaries to Kenya. By the 50's and the 60's, remarkable growth was being experienced as the ministry spread beyond Western Kenya and began to impact communities in the Rift Valley region, Nairobi, Central and Coastal regions, and the Kisii area.

A flagship legacy of PAOC in Kenya is Christ is the Answer Ministries (CITAM), an international ministry that began a little over 50 years ago as a small fellowship targeting the cosmopolitan population of Nairobi. In a previous chapter, I have written in some detail about my involvement with CITAM, which previously operated under the name Nairobi Pentecostal Church.

Under its partnership with the Pentecostal Assemblies of God, PAOC established several supportive ministries that were designed to serve the growing number of churches that were being planted in the region. These ministries included Evangel Publishing House, Pentecostal Bible College and Pan Africa Christian College (PACC), which later became a chartered university.

I had the privilege of contributing in a number of ways toward the development of these three ministries. Let me just share a few anecdotes from my experiences.

Evangel Publishing House

I served as Chairman of Evangel Publishing House (EPH) during the period in which it was moved from Nyang'ori to Nairobi. The move came with a lot of challenges, not least of which was some resistance from the PAG leadership. Another challenge we faced was money. While I was insisting that the publishing house and printing press must move from Nyang'ori to either Kisumu or Nairobi, I was told by Rev. Arnold Bowler, who was then the General Manager, that there was simply no money to facilitate the move.

Not long after we ran into that roadblock, an opportunity arose for me to travel to the U.S. and Canada with Rev. Cal Bombay with the aim of raising funds to enable us to move the printing press to Nairobi. Cal was an amazing negotiator, and he was able to somehow negotiate deals with airlines that left people shaking their heads in wonder.

The trip actually had a double agenda. The first was to raise funds for the EPH move, and the second was to raise funds to enable the Nairobi Pentecostal Church to buy a house for the Pastor. Some of challenges we faced in our attempt to secure a local bank loan for the house were mentioned in a previous chapter. As church Secretary, I took on the responsibility of looking for alternative ways of funding what we felt then was an important facility for the NPC, a church parsonage.

The trip with Cal took us to several cities in the United States where we visited a number of funding agencies including Word Vision in California. The World Vision Director in Kenya had told us that the organization would not be able to give funds for the EPH move, but Cal had insisted on going to their headquarters to make the appeal nonetheless. To my surprise, we were given the funding that we requested.

From California, we flew to the PAOC Headquarters to see Rev. Bill Cornelius, with whom I had developed a close friendship during his tenure as PAOC Field Director. At the time of our visit, he was serving as the Executive Director of Overseas Missions.

The day after we arrived, Bill organized a meeting with the PAOC Finance Committee where I was given an opportunity to present our case. It was a difficult meeting because we were asking PAOC to enter into a loan agreement with NPC, an unprecedented move, the long term implications of which were not clear. At the end of the meeting, the Committee agreed to the request, and a decision was made in good faith to wire the money to Nairobi as requested.

Years later, in 1990, Rev. Gerald Morrison, the then Field Director, convinced me to come out of retirement to take up management of EPH for a few years. EPH was facing financial problems at the time and needed a mature, steady hand of leadership. I believe Rev. Morrison felt that I was the person to guide the publishing house out of the quagmire it was in.

I accepted the job and ended up serving as EPH General Manager for a period of five years. Among the things we did during that period was to dispose of the entire printing side of the business. EPH had old equipment which had been difficult and costly to maintain, and the Board felt that it was time for EPH to focus on being a publisher and not a printer. It was difficult to have to lay off workers, some of whom had been with EPH for decades. But taking this decision certainly did result in the establishment of a viable publishing house.

Pentecostal Bible College

The first PAOC Bible School was started at Goibei in Western Kenya in 1947 under a missionary, Mark Bright. At that time, PAOC was beginning to focus on theological education as a core part of its mission. In 1948, the Bible School was moved to Nyang'ori under the name Bethel Bible College. A year later, in 1949, the name was changed to Pentecostal Bible College (PBC). The first Principal of PBC was a missionary pastor called Rev. John Kitts who was assisted by Pastor Shem Irangi. Pastor Irangi took over as Principal of the School in 1954.

Rev. Kitts, an Englishman, and his wife Sophie took over leadership in the same year that I would be joining Nyang'ori Junior Secondary School as a teacher. Some forty years later, I joined the Board of Governors of PBC, and I served for a number of years on the Board's Disciplinary and Recruitment Committees.

I recall that Sophie was a great singer and was frequently on the radio. At some point, she approached the Government-run radio station, the Voice of Kenya, and asked to be given a weekly program. This request was approved, and Sophie became a well-known voice on national radio.

When the Kitts left the country, the broadcasting equipment that Sophie had been using was left at PBC where, unfortunately, it was not being utilized. The Nairobi Pentecostal Church asked PBC for the equipment, which was then donated to the church. I believe that this was the seed that would later germinate and become what is today the Hope FM ministry.

Pan Africa Christian University

PAOC founded Pan Africa Christian College (PACC) in 1978, initially as a Bible College. The College opened for classes on 2 May 1978 with six students, and it has grown to a student body of over 300 today. A decade or so after it was started, PAC submitted an application to the Commission for Higher Education for accreditation as a fully-fledged university. PAC University was officially awarded a charter on 15 February 2008 by Hon. Mwai Kibaki, the President of Kenya.

My association with the University goes back to its very inception. By God's grace, I was able to make a contribution as a Board member and Advisor at various stages of its growth. It was a privilege to work alongside so many others who have laboured over the years to make PACU the successful institution that it is today.

PAOC Missionaries who Served in Kenya

Through my long association with PAOC, I must say that this organization has had a profound impact on my life. I want to believe that God also used me to contribute meaningfully to the work of PAOC in East Africa. Looking back now, I cannot help but ponder the many personal encounters and relationships that emerged from this association. When all is said and done, it is really the people that matter; not money or projects or achievements.

It is for this reason that I want to dedicate this chapter to honor the many missionaries who came to Kenya at different times and left a mark in my life and the lives of countless others. With the help of a number of friends, particularly Mrs. Marg Foreman who now lives in

Canada, I have compiled a list of the PAOC missionaries who served in Kenya from the time this ministry began to work in Kenya up to the present. The list is much longer than I imagined. May God continue to bless the work of their hands into eternity.

List of PAOC Missionaries Serving in Kenya Since 1942

Yr to Kenya	LAST NAME	FIRST NAMES	TITLE	COMMENTS
1992	Adams	Barbara		
1980	Anderson	Carl & Elizabeth		Radio & Recording Studio, NPC
1979	Angus	Elizabeth		
1984	Anonby	John & Elizabeth	Dr.	
1988	Arbour	Suzanne		
1983	Barrett	Diane		
1960	Batterman	Heinz & Edelgard	Rev.	EPH/Maji Moto
1987	Bear	Robert & Betty		Guest House?
1984	Benjamin	Shanty		
1988	Bennett	Dan		
1985	Berg	Lorraine	Ms	
1991	Bergman	Gordon & Jennie		PACC
	Birch	Ken & Shirley	Dr.	Regional Director
1991	Bjurling	Patrick	Rev.	
1985	Black	Philip & Cynthia		
1962	Bombay	Cal & Mary	Rev.	EPH
1959	Bombay	Richard & Olive	Rev.	NPC/...
1976	Bond	Bill & Margaret	Rev.	PBC
1952	Boris	Irene		
1979	Bowering	Joy		
1955	Bowler	Arnold & Elsie	Rev.	EPH/Malindi

Yr to Kenya	LAST NAME	FIRST NAMES	TITLE	COMMENTS
	Bowler	Kathryn	Ms.	Goibei
1977	Brand	Bruce & Martha	Rev.	EPH
1978	Brndjar	Rodger		
1983	Burry	Barbara		
1974	Bush	Marilyn	Ms.	Medical work; TCL
	Butler	Horace & Elsie	Rev.	
1950	Cantwell	Margaret	Ms.	Kerari, PBC
1968	Carlson	Allan & Joanne		Nyeri/PBC
1975	Chalmers	Kervin & Audrey	Rev.	
1964	Chiarelli	Eli & Elsa	Rev.	Nyang'ori/Embu
1939	Clarke	Fred & Rhoda		
1981	Clarke	Brian & Shelley		
1955	Cornelius	William & Lillian	Rev.	(Warkentin)
1984	Cornelius	Myrrl & Ethel	Rev.	PACC/NPC
1959	Cummins	Dale & Alberta	Rev.	
1981	Curr	Andrea		
	Davis	Roy & Gerda	Rev.	
1987	Dawson	Arlene	Ms.	Teachers Program
1980	Dawson-North	George & Elizabeth		
1949	Deacon	June	Ms.	
1987	Delviken	Evangeline	Ms.	Teachers Program
1991	Dewald	Lisa	Ms.	
1966	Dodding	Richard & Arlene	Rev.	Kisii/Kerari
1985	Douglas	Melvin	Mr.	Mechanic
1955	Dudgeon	Emily		
1965	Duncalfe	Jack & Anne	Rev.	Field Director/PBC
1957	Edler	Mary	Ms.	
1987	Eling	Clarice	Ms.	Maji Moto
1987	Embree	James	Mr.	Teachers Program
1986	Esther	Cechetto	Ms.	

Yr to Kenya	LAST NAME	FIRST NAMES	TITLE	COMMENTS
1981	Evers	Connie (Buzikievich)	Ms.	EPH?
1978	Farrow	Heather		
1993	Faught	Harry & Barbara	Rev.	
1971	Foreman	Garry & Marg	Rev.	PBC, PACC
1950	Francis	Ernest & Shirley	Rev.	
1960	Franz	Martin & Hilde	Rev.	Eldoret/Turkana
1988	Franz	Peter & Rebekkah	Rev.	Gospel Fire International Crusades
1988	Frey	Cornelia		
	Friesen	Eva	Ms.	PACU Librarian/ TELTAC
1984	Friesen	Duff & Therese		
1971	Funk	Betty	Ms.	
1967	Garden	Rae (Schmautz)	Ms.	Goibei
	Gingrich	Virgil & Della	Rev.	PBC
1986	Goodman	Victor		
1971	Hacker	Paul & Jeannine		
1958	Hawkes	Paul & Maryann	Rev.	
1985	Hazzard	David & Stacey	Rev.	PACC
1978	Hearn	Gail		
1930	Hendrickson	Nellie	Ms.	Founder, Teachers Trainin School, EPH
1984	Hern	Louise		
1994	Hesp	Harry & Irene		
1980	Higgins	Patrick & Grace	Dr.	Maji Moto - Veterinarian
1989	Hildebrandt	Wilf & Lillian	Dr.	PACC
	Holder	Frank & Dorothy	Rev.	PBC

Yr to Kenya	LAST NAME	FIRST NAMES	TITLE	COMMENTS
1977	Holmes	Miriam		
1965	Horban	Rose		
	Horrill	Lyle & Irene	Rev.	Itibo, Kisii
1963	Houghton	Philip & Audrey	Rev.	NPC
1994	Irwin	Mary Lou		
1972	Janke	Alfons		Builder
1985	Jardine	Edie (Smith)		Field Office
1968	Johnson	Eugene & Lois	Rev.	NPC Pastor after John McBride
	Johnson	Cheryl Ann	Ms.	Field Office
1981	Johnson	Betty Lou (Faa)	Ms.	PBC
	Kauffeldt	Kirk & Shelley	Dr.	PACU
1918	Keller	Otto & Marion		Founder of Nyang'ori Station
	Kells	Linda		Turkana
1978	Kennedy	Terry		PACC Library
1994	Kipp	Stuart & Shelley		
1940	Kitts	John & Sophie	Rev.	Kikuyu & Kisii tribes, translation
1979	Kohls	Paul & Lynn	Dr.	PACU
1983	Kolba	Wanda		
1984	Koop	Dave & Donna	Mr.	EPH
1984	Korpela	Paavo & Marja	Rev.	PBC
1982	Kroeker	Valerie		PBC/PACC
1987	Kubicek	Mary	Ms.	Teachers Program
1976	Kurtz	Bob & Sally	Rev.	Kapsengari/ Teachers Program ?Sp
1966	Labrentz	Arnold & Doreen	Rev.	EPH
1991	Laing	Gerry & Grace	Mr.	Builder
1983	Lalonde	David & Mary		

Yr to Kenya	LAST NAME	FIRST NAMES	TITLE	COMMENTS
1987	Lambier	Douglas	Mr.	Teachers Program
1984	Langdon	Lynette		
1987	Larkin	Deborah		
1979	Lashley	Wendy	Ms.	NPC Children
1976	Lawrence	Geraldine		
1975	Lehotay	Emise	Ms.	Awasi Mission
1987	Leonard	Martha	Ms.	Turkana
1987	Liira	John	Rev.	Mombasa
1979	Lingren	Sandra		
1981	Livingstone	Katherine		
	Lloyd	Bob & Joan	Mr.	PACU – Building
1985	Longman	Clarence		
1981	Loyley	Martin & Sharon	Rev.	EPH
1976	Loyst	Hazel		
1946	Lynn	John & Edna	Rev.	
1973	Lynn	Doug & Lowanna		Bukoma/Mombasa/NPC
1973	Lynn	LaVerne (Tisher)		Goibei
	MacGowan	Ken & Marj	Rev.	Mombasa
1974	MacMinn	Helen	Rev.	EPH/Field Office/PACU (TCL)
1977	Marek	Karel & Herma		
1979	Marsdin	George & Jennie		
1962	Mascher	Hellmut & Elsie	Rev.	Maji Moto
1980	Mast	Bernhard & Elisabeth		
1975	Mayer	Margaret	Ms.	
1983	McAllister	Mamie		
1943	McBride	John & Ella	Rev.	Education/Field Director/Goibei
1977	McBride	Bruce & Pam		
1956	McQuarrie	Gordon & Minnie	Rev.	

Yr to Kenya	LAST NAME	FIRST NAMES	TITLE	COMMENTS
1976	McQuarrie	Ross & Elida	Rev.	PBC?
1983	Meier	Elsbeth		
1958	Meikle	Claude & Jean		
1958	Miller	Gloria (Myles)		
1984	Miller	Penny	Ms.	Komolian, Pokot
1971	Minor	Harold & Maryella	Rev.	Migori/Field Director
1984	Moffat	Shirley		
1972	Molin	Elvir & Lilly		Builder
	Morrison	Gerald & Ruth	Rev.	
1948	Morrison	Wilbur & Ruby	Rev.	
1951	Morrison	Leroy & Eleanor	Rev.	Assisted Vernon, managed EPH
1963	Morrison	Keith & Eleanor	Rev.	Schools
	Morrison	Vernon & Gertrude	Rev.	Opened the Bible School
1950	Morrison	Eleanor (Malhus)		
1939	Munro	Marion	Ms.	Medical work
1981	Newman	Norman & Janice (Rideout)		Builder (NPC)/ Nurse
1984	Nieuwolt	Simone		
1981	Oldford	Don & Jessie	Rev.	Machakos
1989	Payne	Shivonne		
1989	Petterson	Cynthia		
1989	Phoenix	Kelvin & Jean	Mr.	PACC
1957	Prince	Derek & Lydia	Rev.	
1976	Prosser	Paul & Erika	Rev.	Kapsengari/
1983	Pruden	Nancy		
	Ratz	Calvin & Ruth	Rev.	EPH
1973	Raymer	Bob & Marilyn	Mr.	Kerari Girls
	Raymer	Bonnie (Sawler)	Ms.	Harambee Schools

Yr to Kenya	LAST NAME	FIRST NAMES	TITLE	COMMENTS
1975	Raymer	Ivan & Ada	Rev.	PBC
1968	Reath	James & Judy		
1968	Regehr	Frieda	Ms.	
1984	Reid	Janel	Ms.	
1975	Richard	Davidson		
1978	Richards	James	Dr.	PACC
1987	Richardson	Donna	Ms.	
1965	Ros	Herbert & Christiane	Rev.	
1982	Rosborough	Daniel & Dale		
1951	Rosenau	Arthur & Edna	Rev.	Teacher/
1958	Roth	Kathryn		
1984	Rumball	Carolyn		
1980	Ruthven	Jon	Dr.	PACC
	Sanders	Roy & Margaret	Mr.	Builder
1972	Schaaf	Richard & Frieda		EPH
1954	Scheel	Iris	Rev. ?	A leader in Christian education and curriculum development
1987	Schindel	Reuben & Margaret	Mr.	EPH
1983	Schmale	John & Eleanor	Mr.	Guest house/ Building/etc.
1985	Schmidt	Douglas		
1970	Schneider	Harry & Eleanor (Strom)	Mr.	Field Office
1969	Seaboyer	Bob & Amy	Rev.	Goibei
1988	Shank	Clare & Edna		
1962	Sharp	Bill & Carol		
1954	Shaw	Geoffrey & Pauline (Vaters)		
1939	Siemens	Renata	Ms	Medical work

Yr to Kenya	LAST NAME	FIRST NAMES	TITLE	COMMENTS
1968	Sirett	Carol		Goibei
1983	Sirjoosingh	Deborah	Ms.	Turkana – medical
1936	Skinner	James & Lila	Rev.	Education; supervisor of program
	Skinner	Robert & Doris	Rev.	
1986	Smith	Clayton & Marilyn (Ernst)		Field Office/NPC/PACC
1981	Sohnchen	Ernst & Lydia	Mr.	Field Office
1969	Spengler	Ernst & Denise		
1954	Stevens	Fred J.		
1968	Stevenson	Gerald & Ellen	Rev.	Mombasa
1982	Stoik	Ruth (Anaya)		PACC
1989	Strelau	Anita		
1970	Thomas	Mervyn & Sheila	Rev.	NPC Valley Road
1989	Tollefson	Gordon & Doris	Mr.	EPH
1990	Toman	Deborah		
1982	Tracy	Janice (Newman)		EPH
1990	Tuck	Deborah		Medical
1968	Twigg	Paul & Marjorie		
1979	Underhill	Pamela		
1983	Upton	Roy & Maisie	Rev.	NPC Valley Road
	Verge	Carl & Marian	Dr.	PACU
1985	Vogt	Peter & Maria		
1994	Wall	Susan		
1991	Walters	Timothy & Elaine		
1975	Warkentin	Peter & Evelyn	Mr.	Field Office/Guest House
1985	Warkentin	Jack & Eunice	Mr.	PACC
1979	Watkins	Lewis & Ruth	Rev.	Thika, Central Province

Yr to Kenya	LAST NAME	FIRST NAMES	TITLE	COMMENTS
1982	Weiler	Steve	Mr.	Mechanic
1961	Werbiski	Alvin & Lil	Re.	
1979	Werbiski	Tim		
1983	Weslosky	Eunice		
1986	Weston	Deborah		
1987	White	Dennis & Esther	Rev.	NPC: Valley Road/ Karen

ABOUT THE AUTHOR

Richard Ondeng' describes himself first and foremost as an educator. He began his career as a teacher and rose to become an influential and highly respected education professional in Kenya.

Richard was born in what is now Siaya County and attended Church Missionary Society primary schools in Usingo and Ng'iya. From there, he went to Nyang'ori Junior Secondary School and then Maseno School. Following high school, he enrolled in Kagumo Teachers' College in Nyeri where he trained as a teacher.

Richard began his teaching career in January 1949 at his old school – Nyang'ori, where he served as both teacher and headmaster until December 1956. From January 1957 to December 1960, he worked as a supervisor of schools for the Education Department of the Christian Council of Kenya (CCK), which later became the National Council of Churches of Kenya (NCCK). The Education Department in which Richard worked would eventually become an independent organization called Christian Churches Education Association (CCEA).

His assignment with CCK was in North Nyanza District, which at that time included what later became Western Province. He headed the team that was responsible for managing and supervising all the schools established by the five NCCK member churches working in that district.

From January 1960 to August 1963, Mr. Ondeng' worked as the CCEA Regional Education Secretary for Nyanza Province, which at the time comprised the whole of what later became Nyanza and Western Provinces plus Kericho District. In this position, he coordinated the work of nine District Secretaries with over 900 schools.

From September 1963 to September 1966, Richard was in the United States where he graduated from Goshen College in Indiana with a Bachelor's Degree in English and History.

When he returned from this study leave in 1966, Richard was appointed the CCEA Secretary General and moved to Nairobi. From September 1979 until May 1983, he held two positions, the CCEA Secretary General and NCCK Deputy General Secretary. He resigned from the former in 1983, but continued to serve another eight years as the NCCK Deputy General Secretary. In 1990, he came out of retirement to take on a five-year assignment as the General Manager of Evangel Publishing House (EPH).

Richard Ondeng' married Dinah Rose Auma on 5th January, 1957. They are still sharing life together. Richard and Dinah have eight children – Rhoda Wilhelmsen, Pete Ondeng', Mary Ewing, Karin Worthington, Paul Ondeng', Jim Ondeng', Timothy Ondeng' and Philip Ondeng'. They have 19 grandchildren and one great grandchild.